International Labour and Employment Compliance Handbook

www.kluwerlawonline.com

Labour and Employment Compliance in England

International Bar Association

Labour and Employment Compliance in England

Sixth Edition

Tony Hyams-Parish

This publication is part of the International Labour and Employment Compliance Handbook, available on www.kluwerlawonline.com

Editors: Salvador del Rey and Robert J. Mignin

the global voice of the legal profession

Wolters Kluwer

Published by:
Kluwer Law International B.V.
PO Box 316
2400 AH Alphen aan den Rijn
The Netherlands
E-mail: international-sales@wolterskluwer.com
Website: lrus.wolterskluwer.com

Sold and distributed in North, Central and South America by:
Wolters Kluwer Legal & Regulatory U.S.
7201 McKinney Circle
Frederick, MD 21704
United States of America
Email: customer.service@wolterskluwer.com

Sold and distributed in all other countries by:
Air Business Subscriptions
Rockwood House
Haywards Heath
West Sussex
RH16 3DH
United Kingdom
Email: international-customerservice@wolterskluwer.com

Printed on acid-free paper.

ISBN 978-94-035-0403-2

e-Book: ISBN 978-94-035-0404-9
web-PDF: ISBN 978-94-035-0405-6

Printed in the United Kingdom.

All listed titles are also available on lrus.wolterskluwer.com

1. Argentina: Julio César Stefanoni Zani & Enrique Alfredo Betemps, *Labour and Employment Compliance in Argentina, 6th edition*, 2018 (ISBN 978-94-035-0373-8)
2. Australia: John Tuck, Stephen Price, Rosemary Roach, Jack de Flamingh, Nicholas Ellery & Nick Le Mare, *Labour and Employment Compliance in Australia, 3rd edition*, 2018 (ISBN 978-94-035-0380-6)
3. Belgium: Chris Van Olmen, *Labour and Employment Compliance in Belgium, 3rd edition*, 2018 (ISBN 978-94-035-0383-7)
4. Brazil: Rodrigo Seizo Takano, Andrea Giamondo Massei Rossi & Murilo Caldeira Germiniani, *Labour and Employment Compliance in Brazil, 5th edition*, 2018 (ISBN 978-94-035-0390-5)
5. Canada: Kevin Coon & Adrian Ishak, *Labour and Employment Compliance in Canada, 2nd edition*, 2014 (ISBN 978-90-411-5637-2)
6. Chile: Gerardo Otero A., Maria Dolores Echeverria F., Macarena López M. & María de los Ángeles Fernández S., *Labour and Employment Compliance in Chile, 6th edition*, 2018 (ISBN 978-94-035-0393-6)
7. China: King & Wood Mallesons, *Labour and Employment Compliance in China, 5th edition*, 2018 (ISBN 978-94-035-0400-1)
8. England: Tony Hyams-Parish, *Labour and Employment Compliance in England, 6th edition*, 2018 (ISBN 978-94-035-0403-2)
9. France: Pascale Lagesse, *Labour and Employment Compliance in France, 6th edition*, 2018 (ISBN 978-94-035-0410-0)
10. Germany: Gerlind Wisskirchen & Martin Lützeler, *Labour and Employment Compliance in Germany, 6th edition*, 2018 (ISBN 978-94-035-0413-1)
11. India: Manishi Pathak, *Labour and Employment Compliance in India, 6th edition*, 2018 (ISBN 978-94-035-0420-9)
12. Ireland: Duncan Inverarity & Sinéad Grace, *Labour and Employment Compliance in Ireland, 5th edition*, 2018 (ISBN 978-94-035-0423-0)
13. Israel: Yaron Horovitz, Pnina Broder-Manor & Helen Raziel, *Labour and Employment Compliance in Israel, 5th edition*, 2018 (ISBN 978-94-035-0430-8)
14. Italy: Angelo Zambelli, *Labour and Employment Compliance in Italy, 6th edition*, 2018 (ISBN 978-94-035-0433-9)
15. Japan: Yoshikazu Sugino, *Labour and Employment Compliance in Japan, 6th edition*, 2018 (ISBN 978-94-035-0440-7)
16. Republic of Korea: Sang Wook Cho, Soojung Lee & Christopher Mandel, *Labour and Employment Compliance in the Republic of Korea, 4th edition*, 2018 (ISBN 978-94-035-0453-7)
17. Mexico: Oscar De La Vega Gómez, *Labour and Employment Compliance in Mexico, 6th edition*, 2018 (ISBN 978-94-035-0443-8)
18. The Netherlands: Els de Wind & Cara Pronk, *Labour and Employment Compliance in the Netherlands, 4th edition*, 2018 (ISBN 978-94-035-0470-4)
19. Poland: Barbara Jóźwik, *Labour and Employment Compliance in Poland, 6th edition*, 2018 (ISBN 978-94-035-0450-6)

20. Russia: Anna-Stefaniya Chepik, *Labour and Employment Compliance in Russia*, 2013 (ISBN 978-90-411-4925-1)
21. Saudi Arabia: Sara Khoja & Sarit Thomas, *Labour and Employment Compliance in Saudi Arabia, 1st edition,* 2018 (ISBN 978-94-035-0490-2)
22. South Africa: Susan Stelzner, Stuart Harrison, Brian Patterson & Zahida Ebrahim, *Labour and Employment Compliance in South Africa, 6th edition*, 2018 (ISBN 978-94-035-0460-5)
23. Spain: Salvador del Rey & Ana Campos, *Labour and Employment Compliance in Spain, 6th edition*, 2018 (978-94-035-0463-6)
24. Turkey: Sertaç Kökenek & Elif Nur Çakır, *Labour and Employment Compliance in Turkey, 4th edition*, 2018 (ISBN 978-94-035-0473-5)
25. United Arab Emirates: Sara Khoja & Sarit Thomas, *Labour and Employment Compliance in the United Arab Emirates, 5th edition*, 2018 (ISBN 978-94-035-0480-3)
26. United States: Baker & McKenzie LLP, *Labour and Employment Compliance in the United States, 4th edition*, 2018 (ISBN 978-94-035-0483-4)

International Bar Association
The Global Voice of the Legal Profession

The International Bar Association (IBA), established in 1947, is the world's leading organization of international legal practitioners, bar associations and law societies. The IBA influences the development of international law reform and shapes the future of the legal profession throughout the world. It has a membership of over 40,000 individual lawyers and almost 200 bar associations and law societies spanning all continents. It has considerable expertise in providing assistance to the global legal community.

Grouped into two divisions – the Legal Practice Division and the Public and Professional Interest Division – the IBA covers all practice areas and professional interests, providing members with access to leading experts and up-to-date information. Through the various committees of the divisions, the IBA enables an interchange of information and views among its members as to laws, practices and professional responsibilities relating to the practice of business law around the globe. Additionally, the IBA's high-quality publications and world-class conferences provide unrivalled professional development and network-building opportunities for international legal practitioners and professional associates.

The IBA's Bar Issues Commission provides an invaluable forum for IBA member organisations to discuss all matters relating to law at an international level.

The IBA's Human Rights Institute (IBAHRI) works across the Association, to promote, protect and enforce human rights under a just rule of law, and to preserve the independence of the judiciary and the legal profession worldwide.

Other institutions established by the IBA include the Southern Africa Litigation Centre and the International Legal Assistance Consortium.

Employment and Industrial Relations Law Committee

The aims of the committee are to develop and exchange knowledge of employment and industrial relations law and practice. Members support each other through the provision of innovative ideas and practical assistance on day-to-day issues. In addition, through its journal and through presentations, conferences, the committee ensures the dissemination of up-to-date law and practice in this highly important business area.

International Bar Association Global Employment Institute

The IBA Global Employment Institute (IBA GEI) was formed in early 2010 for the purpose of developing for multinationals and worldwide institutions a global and strategic approach to the key legal issues in the human resources and human capital fields.

Drawing on the resources and expertise of the IBA membership, the IBA GEI will provide a unique contribution in the field of employment, discrimination and immigration law, on a diverse range of global issues, to private and public organizations throughout the world. The IBA GEI is designed to enhance the management, performance and productivity of these organizations and help achieve best practice in their human capital and management functions from a strategic perspective.

The IBA GEI will become the leading voice and authority on global HR issues by virtue of having a number of the world's leading labour and employment practitioners in its ranks, and the support and resource of the world's largest association of international lawyers.

Further information

International Bar Association, 4th Floor, 10 St Bride Street, London EC4A 4AD, United Kingdom, Tel: +44 (0)20 7842 0090, Fax: +44 (0)20 7842 0091, E-mail: member@int-bar.org, www.ibanet.org

About the International Labour and Employment Compliance Handbook

From 1976 through 1988, the International Bar Association and Kluwer Law International published the groundbreaking International Handbook on Contracts of Employment. This Handbook provided one of the first global overviews of the law of the international employment relationship.

Since publishing the first edition, globalization of business has created an increased demand for knowledge of labor and employment laws throughout the world. Therefore, along with Kluwer, we decided to publish an updated Handbook which we have titled the International Labour and Employment Compliance Handbook.

This new Handbook was intended to be a practical guide by providing a general overview of key labor and employment issues in multiple jurisdictions. Each chapter was written so that it is easy to understand by lawyers and non-lawyers alike. Each country author has also followed a standard outline to assist readers in analysing employment issues in each country.

The first edition of this new Handbook included nineteen (19) different countries.

This Handbook would not have been possible without the help and assistance of many people. Most importantly, the individual country authors are all distinguished legal practitioners who spent considerable time drafting and revising their country reports to meet difficult deadlines. We thank each of them. Our friends at Kluwer, especially Ewa Szkatula, have done a wonderful job in keeping the editors and the authors on schedule. Finally,we want to also express our gratitude to Cuatrecasas, Gonçalves Pereira, and Baker & McKenzie LLP for their valuable assistance in the coordination and organization of this project. Our warmest thanks to each of them.

Because of the success of the Handbook,Wolters Kluwer Law & Business decided to publish each country report also as a separate book to give a choice in obtaining the information. We hope this new format will be a helpful and useful resource just like the Handbook. Both formats are available in print and online.

The Editors

Salvador del Rey Guanter
Robert J. Mignin

March 2013

England

AUTHOR

Tony Hyams-Parish

Tony Hyams-Parish is a Partner in the Employment Team at DMH Stallard LLP where he advises a corporate client base, ranging from large multinationals to small owner-managed businesses, on all aspects of employment law. Having qualified into the legal profession as a barrister, Tony has rights of audience in all courts, including Higher Courts, and regularly represents his clients at Employment Tribunals. Tony is continually rated as a leading employment lawyer in Chambers Guide to the Legal Profession and Legal 500 where his expertise in complex employment litigation is widely acknowledged.

ADDRESS

DMH Stallard LLP
6 New Street Square
New Fetter Lane
London
EC4A 3BF

Tel.: +44(0)207 822 1500
Fax: +44(0) 207 842 2333
E-mail: tony.hyams-parish@dmhstallard.com
Web: <www.dmhstallard.com>

Table of Contents

TABLE OF CONTENTS

Legal Compliance in England

1. LEGAL FRAMEWORK: EMPLOYMENT LAWS

Employment law in England has three main sources:

- *Contract*: The relationship between the employer and the employee is governed at common law by the contract of employment.
- *Legislation*: A range of statutes and statutory instruments confer a number of minimum statutory rights on employees, one of the most important of these being the Employment Rights Act 1996 (ERA) which provides, amongst many other rights, a right not to be unfairly dismissed. The Equality Act 2010 (EqA) deals with discrimination law and the Working Time Regulations 1998 (WTR) sets out minimum requirements in terms of maximum working hours, providing holiday, rest breaks, etc.
- *European law*: Employees have acquired additional rights (and employers have acquired additional obligations) as a result of European law, particularly in the areas of discrimination, equal pay and 'family-friendly' rights.[1]

2. CONTRACTS OF EMPLOYMENT

2.1. Overview

A contract of employment need not be in writing and may be partly written and partly oral. Although oral contracts are legally enforceable, it is always better to have a written contract as evidence of the terms that have been agreed between the parties.

---

1. At the time of writing it is not clear what the impact will be of BREXIT on UK employment laws in the longer term. Certainly in the shorter term no changes are anticipated.

A contract of employment will generally consist of:

- Express terms, which are those that have been specifically agreed between the parties, whether in writing or orally;
- Implied terms, which are those that are taken to have been agreed, because:
  (a) they are too obvious to need recording;
  (b) they are part of the custom and practice of the business or industry;
  (c) they can be logically deduced from the conduct of the parties;
  (d) they are necessary to give 'business efficacy' to the agreement as a whole;
- statutory terms those derived from employment legislation;
- terms incorporated into individual contracts from other sources, such as collective agreements.

The terms of employment may be found in one document or a combination of documents, including a staff handbook.

2.2. Written Employment Contracts

Employees who have been employed for one month or more are entitled by section 1 ERA to a written statement of particulars of employment. The written particulars must be provided to employees within two months of starting employment. This document should contain all of terms relating to the following:

- the scale or rate of pay;
- the intervals at which the employee is to be paid (i.e., weekly, monthly or other specified intervals);
- hours of work;
- entitlement to holidays and holiday pay;
- incapacity for work due to sickness or injury, including any provision for sick pay;
- pensions and pension schemes;
- the length of notice which the employee is obliged to give and entitled to receive to terminate his contract of employment;
- the title of the job which the employee is employed to do or a brief description of the work for which he is employed;
- where the employment is not intended to be permanent, the period for which it is expected to continue or, if it is for a fixed term, the date when it is to end;
- either the place of work or, where the employee is required or permitted to work at various places, an indication of that and of the address of the employer;
- any collective agreements which directly affect the terms and conditions of the employment including, where the employer is not a party, the persons by whom they were made;
- where the employee is required to work outside the United Kingdom for a period of more than one month, the period for which he is to work outside

the United Kingdom and the currency in which remuneration is to be paid while he is working outside the United Kingdom;
- any additional remuneration payable to him, and any benefits to be provided to or in respect of him, by reason of his being required to work outside the United Kingdom.

Subject to the above, there is no legal requirement for other contractual terms to be in writing – they may be either written or oral or even a mixture of the two.

If an employer fails to provide a section 1 ERA statement or provides an inaccurate or incomplete statement, an employee may make a claim to the employment tribunal for compensation of up to four weeks' pay.

Unless an employment contract specifically provides for a power to vary, an employer will only be able to change terms of employment with the consent of the employee. If the employee does not consent, an employer has two choices: vary it unlawfully and risk the employee suing for breach of contract; or terminate the old contract and replace it with a new contract on the new terms, with the risk that an employee may claim to have been unfairly dismissed.

2.3. Oral Contracts

Although technically in breach of section 1 ERA, which requires the main terms of a contract to be provided in writing to the employee, oral contracts are as binding as written contracts. However, the inevitable problem with an oral contract is that it may be difficult to prove the exact terms and conditions of the employment. If there is only an oral contract, otherwise extraneous matters, such as job advertisements and representations made at an interview, will have increased significance. The courts have indicated their willingness to use the wording contained in advertisements to interpret ambiguous terms in an oral contract. For all these reasons, it is advisable for employment contracts to be in writing in case of a later dispute regarding the agreed terms.

2.4. Employee Handbooks

It is normal practice for employers to issue employees with a staff handbook. Commonly a staff handbook contains all the non-contractual policies and procedures that are applicable to the employment. The benefit of ensuring that the handbook is non-contractual is so that it can be amended and updated without obtaining the consent of the employees. Occasionally, however, some employers opt to have a contract of employment which is a combination of certain terms set out in a staff handbook together with those terms set out in the individual contract issued to the employee.

2.5. Job Description

There is no obligation to provide an employee with a job description, but an employee's written statement of employment must include the title of the job that the employee is employed to do or a brief description of the work for which s/he is employed.

2.6. Offer Letters

An employer needs to consider whether an offer letter will form part or all of the contractual terms (once accepted by the employee) or whether the employer intends to have a separate more detailed contract of employment that the employee will sign when they start work. If the offer letter is to comprise the entire contract then it is important to check that the offer letter contains all the relevant terms of employment and expressly incorporates any other documents that may contain contractual terms, for example, a staff handbook.

If the offer letter is to be superseded by a more detailed written contract of employment once the employee starts work, then the employer may wish to make the offer of employment conditional upon the signing of the full contract and acceptance of its terms (in other words mark the offer letter 'subject to contract'). This will prevent an employee from arguing that the employer is unilaterally trying to change the terms agreed in their offer letter.

A common problem occurs where the terms of the offer letter and the terms of the subsequent contract of employment are inconsistent. The contract should make it clear that in the event of any inconsistency, it is the contract terms that will prevail. It may also be useful to include an 'entire agreement' clause in the offer letter and/or contract which records that the document contains the entire agreement as to the employee's terms of employment (if this is the case) as this will prevent an employee subsequently arguing that they are entitled to contractual terms other than those set out in the offer letter or contract. For the same reason, it may be advisable to include a provision in the offer letter or contract stating that the employee has not relied on any oral or written representations which are not contained in the offer letter or contract, to head off a misrepresentation claim that, for example, they were promised a particular promotion at interview and that was the reason they accepted the offer of employment.

The employer needs to consider whether the offer of employment should contain any conditions precedent. If these are required they must be clearly set out in the offer letter. Common conditions include:

- the need to obtain an appropriate work permit;
- immigration approval for an employee who does not have permission to work in the UK;
- receipt of references or background checks which are satisfactory to the employer;

- receipt of regulatory or other relevant professional body approval;
- obtaining any qualifications specifically required for the job.

2.7. Checklist of Do's and Don'ts

- Ensure that all employees sign a contract of employment, or at the very least, a basic written statement of terms and conditions that complies with section 1 ERA. Such document should ideally be issued at the start of employment but no later than two months after employment starts.
- Consider including specific terms in the contract of employment that provide some protection against the disclosure of confidential information, poaching clients after the employment has ended, etc.
- Include in an offer letter a number of conditions precedent relating to references, qualifications, right to work in the UK, etc.
- Even if there is no staff handbook in place, ensure that certain procedures, such as disciplinary, grievance and equal opportunities policies and procedures are drafted and made accessible to employees.
- When writing an offer letter, employers should consider what they want to achieve, whether it will form part of the contract of employment or whether a contract will follow, in which case special care will need to be taken to ensure that there are no inconsistencies between the contract and the offer letter.

3. RECRUITING, INTERVIEWING, SCREENING AND HIRING EMPLOYEES

3.1. Overview

Recruitment is an expensive process. A lot of time and money is spent by the employer deciding on the job specifications, advertising the job, engaging recruitment agencies, and finally, interviewing the candidates. Therefore, it is a decision that employers want to get right first time, or else they could end up employing a candidate that is not actually suited for the role, which could potentially be very costly and disruptive to the employer.

3.2. Recruiting

Effective recruitment procedures enable employers to recruit the very best employees while reducing the risks of litigation. Such procedures require an objective, systematic and planned approach to recruitment if unlawful discrimination is to be avoided. Both short-listing and selection should be on the basis of candidates' relevant experience, skills, qualifications, knowledge and talent, and should be based on factual evidence. It is advisable that employers devise and implement recruitment procedures and guidelines for all staff involved in the process of recruitment so as to ensure that these incorporate the principles of equal opportunities. It is also imperative that all those involved in recruitment and selection should be properly trained in recruitment procedures and the principles of equality.

There is no statutory framework specifically governing the recruitment process in England and Wales. However, employers are prohibited from discriminating during the recruitment process, when making the decision as to whether or not to make an offer of employment to a particular applicant, and in relation to the terms of employment offered to the successful applicant. Discrimination is unlawful if it is based on race, colour, nationality, ethnic or national origin, sex, disability, age, religion/belief, sexual orientation, gender re-assignment, pregnancy and maternity, marital or civil partner status and trade union membership. It is also unlawful to discriminate against staff on the grounds of fixed-term or part-time status.

3.3. Employment Applications

The starting point for any job applicant looking for a position with a prospective employer is to submit a written application. The two most common forms of application are the curriculum vitae (with a covering letter) or a standard application form produced by the employer. The advantage of application forms is that the employer can control the type of information that is collected and restrict such information to that which is relevant to the position being applied for. Application forms also ensure that everyone competes at the same level.

3.4. Pre-employment Enquiries

As well as checking out references, an employer may choose to verify factual data provided by the employee such as academic qualifications. The employer may wish to ask to see original certificates, for example, either before an offer is made or as a condition of the offer. Employers have a great deal of discretion when deciding which pre-employment enquiries to make on a prospective employee.

3.5. Pre-employment Tests and Examinations

Many employers require applicants to undertake aptitude tests in order to demonstrate typing, computer skills or other technical skills relevant to the role. Tests should always relate to the skills required to perform the offered employment. Language skills may need to be tested where proficiency in a language is a requirement for a particular role. Care should be taken over assumptions made that applicants from outside the UK or of particular nationalities will or will not be proficient in English.

Employers are increasingly using psychometric testing, which tests aspects of personality and intelligence, or biodata that tests biographical data. Thought needs to be given as to whether tests such as these are necessary and proportionate, will involve any invasion of privacy, how feedback may be given, and how the data generated is to be stored. These tests should not be the sole method of assessment and all candidates will need to be informed in advance, either verbally or in writing, if these are to be used as testing methods.

Section 60(1) of the EqA provides that, other than where the exceptions below apply, a prospective employer must not ask about the health of the applicant before making an offer of employment.

This applies whether the employer asks the question of the applicant or of some other person, such as the applicant's former employer by way of a reference request. Further, the above applies even where an agent or employee of the employer, rather than the employer itself, asks the questions.

The exceptions referred to above can be applied where the questions are necessary for the purpose of any of the following:

- Establishing if the applicant will be able to comply with a requirement to undergo an assessment (i.e., an interview or other process designed to give an indication of the applicant's suitability for the work concerned), or establishing if a duty to make reasonable adjustments is (or will be) imposed on the employer in relation to the applicant in connection with a requirement to undergo an assessment.
- Establishing if the applicant will be able to carry out a function that is intrinsic to the work concerned.
- Monitoring diversity in the range of persons applying to the employer for work.
- Taking action to which section 158 EqA (permitted positive action) would apply if references in that section to persons who share (or do not share) a protected characteristic were references to disabled persons (or persons who are not disabled) and the reference to the characteristic were a reference to disability.
- Where the employer applies a requirement to have a particular disability, establishing whether the applicant has that disability.

A breach of section 60 is an unlawful act for the purposes of the EqA.

3.6. Background, Reference and Credit Checks

Pre-employment credit checks are not prohibited by law but should be proportionate to the role applied for. Credit checks should only be used where there is no less intrusive and reasonably practicable alternative. It is likely to be appropriate to carry out credit checks for a role that involves the prospective employee handling cash or accounts or working for a financial institution (where a bad credit rating could compromise organizational integrity) but not otherwise.

There is no general legal obligation on an employer to provide a reference but there may be a specific obligation in the following situations:

- the employer has made a contractual commitment to provide a reference;
- a failure to provide a reference might amount to unlawful discrimination or victimization;
- a professional body requires that a reference should be provided.

Following up on references from previous employers is an important precaution although it may not always produce a completely satisfactory explanation about an employee's reason for leaving a previous job as the previous employer may be reluctant to provide this information.

There is no express prohibition on an employer asking a job applicant, an employee or worker, or a volunteer about their criminal record. Instead, the law attempts to maintain a balance between:

- Rehabilitating people with criminal records so that they are able to move on with their lives and contribute to the society.
- Recognizing that there is an overriding need for disclosure in certain situations and to protect certain groups from those who have committed certain offences.

For this reason, those job applicants who have convictions that are considered 'spent' within the meaning of the Rehabilitation of Offenders Act 1974 may hold themselves out as having a clean record and do not have to declare such convictions to a prospective employer. There are, however, a number of occupations (e.g., teaching or other work with children) where convictions would never be considered 'spent' and would therefore need to be declared.

Generally, employers cannot readily check whether a prospective employee has convictions. For certain occupations, however, employers can obtain such information using the Disclosure and Barring Service.

3.7. Interviewing

Employers may ask any questions they like at interview provided that they do not ask any potentially discriminatory questions, for example, questions asked of a female candidate that would not be asked of a man, such as those concerned with plans to have children. To avoid the risk of claims of discrimination, it is good practice for interviewers only to ask questions which relate to the candidate's ability to do the job (after reasonable adjustments, if necessary).

3.8. Hiring Procedures

Employers should ensure that employees sign a contract before commencing employment, satisfactory references have been received, checks made regarding qualifications (where appropriate) and that proof has been obtained that employees have a right to work in the United Kingdom.

3.9. Fines and Penalties

If an employer is found to be liable for an act of discrimination they can be ordered to pay compensation to the complainant. There is no limit to the compensation that can be ordered.

An employer will also be liable to a civil penalty if it negligently employs someone who does not have permission to work in the United Kingdom. There is a statutory defence if the employer checks certain documents before the employment starts and (in some cases) at least every twelve months during employment. In addition, an employer will commit a criminal offence if it knowingly employs someone who does not have permission to work in the United Kingdom.

3.10. Checklist of Do's and Don'ts

- Ensure that descriptions and specifications are compiled for every job.
- Consider carefully the criteria or requirements for each role and whether they could potentially have an indirect discriminatory impact or may narrow the pool of candidates who may apply.
- Adopt a system for receiving applications that allows the employer to control the amount and type of information sought, such as a standard application form.
- Adopt a recruitment policy that sets out the procedures to be followed in connection with advertising posts, short-listing, interviewing, etc.
- Consider the pre-employment checks that are necessary for the post being recruited.

4. MANAGING PERFORMANCE/CONDUCT

4.1. Overview

Poor performance and misconduct are both issues that an employer can expect to face from time-to-time with employees. There are no positive duties on employers as to how to handle and manage performance and conduct issues. However, while employers have a great deal discretion in such matters, if an employee is dismissed, s/he may challenge the fairness of that process in the employment tribunal if the employer has not acted fairly and reasonably in dealing with the employee.

Disciplinary and capability procedures enable employers to set a framework within which managers can address and improve conduct and poor performance issues in the workplace.

4.2. Coaching and Counselling

Employees who are formally performance managed will be likely to have received some form of informal coaching and counselling. However, where formal action based on poor performance is taken and results in a disciplinary warning, an employer is under a duty to provide whatever training and assistance that is reasonable in the circumstances, which will help the employee improve. The law doesn't stipulate how much; however, if the employer dismisses on the grounds of capability, the extent to which the employer provided support and assistance is relevant to the fairness of the dismissal.

4.3. Written Evaluations

Many employers have a system of appraisals that assist with the identification of performance issues at an early stage, but there is no legal obligation on them to do so. An appraisal is a two-way process between an employee and employer during which targets and objectives are set – and areas of improvement highlighted.

4.4. Warnings and Suspensions

Except where an employee commits an act of gross misconduct (i.e., conduct which is serious enough to justify immediate dismissal without warnings) or gross negligence, the disciplinary/capability procedure provides a system of warnings, and if such a process is followed, a dismissal is likely to be found to be fair. The ACAS (Advisory, Conciliation and Arbitration Service) code of practice on discipline and grievances at work ('the ACAS code') also sets out minimum standards of good practice for dealing with disciplinary and grievance issues. The system of warnings is not provided by statute, but case law and the ACAS code has confirmed the importance of warnings before dismissing for non-performance/capability or conduct.

In instances of serious misconduct, an employer may wish to suspend the employee who is being investigated. This may be appropriate, for example, where there is a potential threat to the business or to other employees, or when it is not possible to properly investigate the allegation if the employee remains at work (e.g., because the employee may destroy evidence or attempt to influence witnesses). In no other circumstances is suspension likely to be viewed as necessary or normal, and an inappropriate suspension could have serious consequences for an employer. For example, if an employer suspends an employee unnecessarily, it could undermine the mutual trust and confidence between the employer and employee and leave an employee with a right to resign and claim constructive dismissal.

Suspension should be used where necessary to investigate a claim of misconduct or where an employer believes that an employee should not do his/her job until the disciplinary proceedings have been completed, for example, in a case where a teacher is accused of making inappropriate comments to a pupil, suspension may be necessary for child-protection reasons.

4.5. Checklist of Do's and Don'ts

- Conduct regular evaluations of employees to give an honest assessment of their performance and allow them to raise any concerns. Do not give flattering performance reviews if they are undeserved; it could make proving a fair dismissal in the future more difficult.
- Keep accurate records of action, including informal action, taken against employees.
- Don't deal with matters continually on an informal basis and then expect to be able to dismiss without going through a system of formal warnings; it is better to move to a formal process sooner, if informal action is not working.
- When issuing warnings for non-performance, implement a system of reviews, coaching and training in appropriate cases.

5. TERMINATION OF EMPLOYEES FOR PERFORMANCE OR DISCIPLINARY REASONS

5.1. Overview

Employment law in England and Wales protects employees with at least two years' service against being unfairly dismissed. For such employees, a dismissal can only be fair if the reason for dismissal:

- relates to the employee's misconduct;
- relates to the employee's lack of capability or qualifications;
- is due to redundancy;
- is because continuing to employ the employee would be illegal, for example, as a result of their immigration status;
- is for 'some other substantial reason' (SOSR). SOSR may be used where the reason for dismissal does not fall neatly into one of the other potentially fair reasons for dismissal, such as dismissal because a fixed term contract has ended, or dismissal because an employee has refused to accept reasonable changes to his/her contract of employment.

A dismissal for any reason which is not one of the above potentially fair reasons, will be unfair.

In addition to the requirement that any dismissal is for a fair reason, an employer must act reasonably and fairly in treating that reason as a reason for dismissal.

As stated above, it is potentially fair to dismiss an employee for misconduct and poor performance/capability. Misconduct may be either a single act of serious misconduct or a series of acts that are less serious. This could include misconduct such as:

- disobeying reasonable orders;
- breach of certain terms of the contract (including breach of the duties of good faith and mutual trust and confidence);
- theft or dishonesty;
- unauthorized absence from work;
- violence at work;
- alcohol or drug abuse (although this may be treated as an illness);
- disclosure of confidential information, competing or preparing to compete;
- repeated poor attendance.

Most employers include examples of unacceptable misconduct in their employment contracts or staff handbooks.

It may be fair to dismiss an employee for conduct outside the workplace if it affects the employer or could be thought to affect employee performance.

For example, becoming involved in a fight outside work whilst wearing a uniform that would identify the employer or when a teacher is prosecuted for downloading child pornography.

To ensure that a dismissal on the grounds of conduct is fair, the employer must be able to show that, at the time of the dismissal:

- It believed the employee to be guilty of misconduct.
- It had reasonable grounds for believing that the employee was guilty of that misconduct.
- When it formed that belief on those grounds, it had carried out as much investigation as was reasonable in the circumstances.

When deciding if an employer has acted reasonably in dismissing an employee for lack of capability or qualifications, the tribunal will need to consider factors such as:

- whether the employee knew what was required of them;
- whether the employer took steps to minimize the risk of poor performance;
- whether it provided training, supervision and encouragement;
- whether it warned the employee of the consequences of failing to improve;
- whether it gave the employee a chance to improve; and
- in some cases, whether the employer considered alternative employment.

When a determination is made about whether a dismissal is fair, one factor will be whether the employer has followed the ACAS code. As stated above, the ACAS code contains much of what is considered to be good practice for employers.

Generally, employees must have been employed for two years before they can bring a claim for unfair dismissal. However, certain types of dismissals are deemed automatically unfair and employees are protected from day one. These include dismissals for reasons connected to pregnancy, parental leave, requests for flexible work hours and whistleblowing.

5.2. Separation/Severance Pay

Assuming that an employee is dismissed fairly for misconduct, lack of capability, or other reasons, the only liability that will arise when the employment contract is terminated is to provide notice of termination (as defined by the contract of employment) or pay in lieu of such notice, unless the contract allows the employer to dismiss summarily (i.e., without notice) for, for example, gross misconduct or gross negligence.

If an employer has not followed the correct procedure and faces a potential claim of unfair dismissal, it is likely that an agreement will need to be reached with the employee in terms of a severance payment to compensate him/her for the unfair dismissal if a tribunal claim is to be avoided. In these circumstances, if a settlement is agreed, the employee should be asked to sign a compromise agreement, effectively waiving any further rights to bring employment claims against the employer.

5.3. Fines and Penalties

If an employee is unfairly dismissed, a claim can be made to the employment tribunal, and the employer may be ordered to pay compensation. The maximum compensation that can be awarded for unfair dismissal is the lower of twelve months' salary or the statutory cap. Compensation may also be increased by up to 25% where the employer has breached the ACAS code, subject to the above maximum.[2]

5.4. Checklist of Do's and Don'ts

- Adopt a comprehensive disciplinary and capability procedure setting out the correct procedure to be followed when an employee is faced with disciplinary and performance management issues.
- Include a non-exhaustive list of examples of gross misconduct, either in the disciplinary procedure or contract of employment permitting the employer to summarily dismiss (i.e., dismiss without notice).
- Adopt a system of regular appraisals that will assist an employer to identify, and act on, poor performance issues at an early stage.
- Except in cases of gross misconduct and gross negligence, do not dismiss an employee with two year's service unless s/he has formally been warned that if the poor performance or conduct continues, dismissal will follow.
- Conduct a thorough investigation and carry out a fair process prior to dismissing employees for misconduct or capability in respect of employees with two year's service or more.
- Be aware of any discriminatory issues because employees need not have accumulated any length of service to claim that a dismissal is discriminatory.
- Check that the reason for dismissal does not fall within one of the categories of dismissal that do not have a two year's service requirement.
- Keep good records of all action taken against employees on the grounds of poor performance and misconduct.

2. As of 6 Apr. 2018 the statutory cap is GBP 83,682 and is reviewed, and generally increased, each year.

6. LAYOFFS, REDUCTIONS IN FORCE, AND/OR REDUNDANCIES AS A RESULT OF JOB ELIMINATIONS OR OTHER RESTRUCTURING

6.1. Overview

Employers making twenty or more redundancies are subject to the rules on collective consultation. Breach of the collective consultation provisions can give rise to separate claims and penalties over and above those arising from any unfair dismissal.

6.2. Reductions in Force/Layoffs/Job Eliminations

Definition of Redundancy

An employer can make employees redundant in any one of three circumstances:
- There is a closure of the business.
- There is a closure of the part of the site or location where an employee is employed to work.
- There is a reduced requirement for an employee to carry out work of a particular kind.

Unfair Redundancy

In order to ensure that a dismissal for redundancy is fair, an employer must establish that:

- redundancy is the real reason for the dismissal; and
- the employer acted reasonably, in all the circumstances of the case, in treating redundancy as the reason for dismissing the employee.

In practice, acting reasonably and fairly requires that a fair procedure has been followed. When considering reasonableness, an employment tribunal will consider whether the steps taken by an employer in dismissing an employee fell within the range of conduct that a reasonable employer could have adopted.

An employer will normally not act reasonably in relation to redundancies (and a dismissal will therefore be unfair) unless it:

- warns and consults employees, or their representative(s), about the proposed redundancies;
- adopts a fair basis upon which to select employees for redundancy (An employer must identify the correct pool from which to select potentially redundant employees and must select employees using proper criteria);
- considers suitable alternative employment (An employer must offer suitable alternative employment within its organization if it is available).

In order to consult properly, an employer must have an open mind and still be capable of being influenced about the matters that form the subject matter of consultation. This suggests that consultation will only be meaningful if it happens at a formative stage. It has been said that fair consultation involves giving employees fair and proper opportunity to understand fully the matters about which they are being consulted and to express their views on those subjects, with the employer thereafter considering those views properly and genuinely.

The matters that should be discussed during the consultation process will depend on the specific circumstances but, typically, fair consultation will include:

- an opportunity for the employee to comment on the basis for selection, both in terms of the pool and the selection criteria;
- an opportunity for the employee to challenge their redundancy selection assessment and to explain any factors that might have led to their selection and of which their employer might not have been aware;
- an opportunity for the employee to put forward suggestions about ways to avoid their redundancy;
- consideration of any alternative employment positions that may exist; and
- an opportunity for the employee to address any other matters or concerns that they may have.

Unless an employer is obliged to engage in collective consultation (as described below) there are no prescribed timescales within which consultation should take place, but the shorter the consultation, the more likely it is that the quality of the consultation will be called into question. If an employee is not consulted until late in the redundancy process, a tribunal will be particularly concerned about the adequacy of the consultation.

In order to be reasonable, selection criteria must, as far as possible, be both objective and capable of independent verification. This means that the criteria should be measurable rather than based on someone's personal opinion.

Potentially fair selection criteria might include:

- performance and ability;
- length of service;
- attendance records; and
- disciplinary records.

Collective Consultation

There is a duty to collectively consult where an employer proposes to dismiss as redundant twenty or more employees at one establishment within a period of ninety days or less. For these purposes, the definition of 'dismiss as redundant' is slightly wider than the standard definition of redundancy (see Definition of Redundancy above) and means any termination of an employment contract where the reason for the dismissal does not relate to the individual employee concerned. Such definition would bring not only traditional redundancy dismissals within its scope but also dismissals, for example, where an employer proposes to dismiss employees who have not agreed to a change to their contracts of employment.

The duty is to inform and consult appropriate representatives of the 'affected employees'. Where the duty applies, the employer must also notify the Secretary of State of the proposed redundancies. Failure to do so is a criminal offence.

'Affected employees' are those affected by the proposed dismissals or by measures which the employer proposes to take in connection with the dismissals. Where any of the affected employees fall into a category in respect of which a trade union is recognized, the trade union must be consulted. In other cases, the employer may consult with representatives directly elected by the affected employees or with an appropriate standing body of representatives elected or appointed for some other purpose, such as an existing works council or other employee body elected to represent employees.

Where elected representatives are required, there are specific statutory rules governing the election and the adequacy of representation produced by that election.

Certain minimum time periods for the consultation apply, depending on the scale of the redundancies proposed. Where 100 or more redundancies are proposed, consultation must begin at least forty-five days before the first dismissal takes effect. For less than 100 but more than 20 redundancies, the consultation period has to begin thirty days before the first dismissal.

Consultation begins with the provision of information (specified by statute) on the proposals to representatives. As a minimum, consultation must be undertaken with a view to reaching agreement on ways to avoid the dismissals, reduce the number of dismissals and mitigate their consequences. It is generally not sufficient for the employer to simply explain its proposals and listen to any counter-proposals.

Whenever there is an obligation to consult collectively, the employer will still need to ensure that it has followed a fair procedure in relation to individuals, including consulting with them properly, so as to minimize claims for unfair dismissal.

Alternatives to Redundancy: Lay-Offs and Short-Time Working

As an alternative to making employees redundant, an employer may wish to deal with an unexpected downturn in its business or unforeseen circumstances by laying off employees or putting them on short-time working, that is, requiring employees to work fewer hours than they are contracted for – commonly a four, three or even a two day week.

Some employers anticipate the need to lay off employees or to put them on short-time working by including an express right to do so in employment contracts. Others operate within industries where, through custom and practice of laying off employees or putting them on short-time working, the employer has an implied right to do so.

If an employer lays off an employee or puts them on short-time working in the absence of an express or implied right to do so, the employer will be in fundamental breach of contract, entitling the employee to resign and claim constructive dismissal. If the reason for dismissal is redundancy, which is probable in this situation, the employee may also claim a statutory redundancy payment. Alternatively, an employee with insufficient service to bring a redundancy pay or unfair dismissal claim, or who does not wish to do so, may remain in employment and claim any shortfall in wages by means of a deduction from wages claim.

6.3. Fines and Penalties

Redundancy Payments

Employees with a least two years' continuous employment are entitled to a statutory redundancy payment if they are dismissed by reason of redundancy.

Statutory redundancy pay is calculated according to a formula based on age, length of service and pay. The maximum number of years that may be taken into account to calculate a redundancy payment is twenty years. Further, for these purposes, a week's pay is capped at the statutory maximum, currently GBP 508.00.[3]

Unfair Dismissal

Employees with two year's continuous service or more can bring a claim of unfair dismissal if their employer has acted unreasonably in making them redundant. In practice, complaints will generally be about a lack of consultation, failure to follow a fair procedure and not offering alternative jobs where available. The maximum compensation that can be awarded by an employment tribunal for unfair dismissal is the lower of twelve months' salary or the statutory cap.

Breach of Collective Consultation Procedures

Failure to comply with any of the rules on information or consultation, or on the election of representatives, can lead to a *protective award* being made by an employment tribunal. The maximum protective award is up to ninety days' pay per dismissed employee. This is gross pay and the statutory cap on

3. Figure correct as at 6 Apr. 2017. This sum increases each year.

a week's pay does not apply. The award is not based on loss of earnings, but on the seriousness of the employer's default.

Failure to Notify the Secretary of State

Failure to provide the notification of collective redundancies to the Secretary of State is a criminal offence and an employer will be liable on summary conviction to an unlimited fine.

6.4. Checklist of Do's and Don'ts

- Identify the number of proposed redundancies at an early stage so that the correct procedures can be adopted.
- Plan the redundancy process carefully, but be prepared to be flexible if necessary.
- Think carefully about trying to avoid the collective consultation obligations by making small groups of employees redundant (i.e., less than twenty employees) within a short time of each other. Employment tribunals will be alert to such tactics and may conclude that it was always known that the later redundancies would be made and that the collective consultation procedures should therefore have been applied.
- Allow sufficient time for meaningful consultation. Discuss the reasons for the redundancies as well as other issues such as selection.
- Consider carefully the appropriate pool of employees from which selections for redundancy are to be made, ensuring that the pool comprises, not only those employees doing the same job, but possibly other employees who do a similar job or have similar skill sets.
- Give careful thought to selection criteria. Do not use criteria which are too subjective, or which might indirectly discriminate on the grounds of sex or disability.

7. LABOUR AND EMPLOYMENT LAW RAMIFICATIONS UPON THE ACQUISITION OR SALE OF A BUSINESS

7.1. Overview

An acquisition or sale of a business is likely to be subject to the Transfer of Undertakings (Protection of Employment) Regulations 2006 (TUPE). The effect of TUPE is that all the employees employed in the business at the point of acquisition or sale are transferred to the buyer under their existing terms of employment. Before the introduction of TUPE, and if TUPE does not apply, employees' contracts often terminated upon the sale of a business.

7.2. Acquisition of a Business

TUPE applies to a 'relevant transfer', which is defined under TUPE as either:

- a transfer of a business, undertaking or part of a business or undertaking where there is a transfer of an economic entity that retains its identity (a 'business transfer'); or
- a client engaging a contractor to do work on its behalf, re-assigning such a contract or bringing the work 'in-house' (a 'service provision change').

TUPE does not apply to a transfer of shares, although it would apply to an asset transfer carried out as a precursor to a share sale to ensure that the relevant assets are contained in, or removed from, the corporate entity whose shares are to be sold. There may also be a transfer of the business or part of the business to a holding company following a share transfer.

The Automatic Transfer Principle

Where there is a TUPE transfer, employees employed by the seller and 'assigned to the grouping of employees that is subject to the relevant transfer' will transfer to the buyer under their existing terms of employment and with their continuity of employment unbroken. This includes anyone employed in the grouping immediately before the transfer and anyone who would have been so employed if they had not been dismissed because of the transfer or a reason connected with it.

TUPE does not transfer any employees who are only temporarily assigned to the grouping. Whether an assignment is 'temporary' will depend on a number of factors, which may include the length of the assignment and whether a date has been set for the employee's return or re-assignment to another part of the business or undertaking.

Self-employed consultants working under a contract for services are generally not covered by TUPE.

Those employed by a service company or holding company but who provide their services wholly or mainly to the undertaking (or part) transferred are not automatically transferred to the buyer. This provides a way for employers to circumvent TUPE by ensuring that the employees working in a business are technically employed by someone other than the legal entity that actually owns the business (or part) being transferred.

Rights in Connection with the Contracts

All of the seller's rights, powers, duties and liabilities under or in connection with the transferring employees' contracts pass to the buyer and any acts or omissions of the seller before the transfer are treated as having been done by the buyer. In other words, there is a statutory novation of employment contracts and the buyer steps into the seller's shoes in respect of all the employees working in the organized grouping at the moment of transfer.

The transfer of all existing rights, duties, liabilities and obligations highlights the need for due diligence by the buyer to ascertain exactly what accrued liabilities and obligations it is acquiring.

Accrued Liabilities

All accrued liabilities of the seller, such as acts and omissions which can give rise to constructive dismissal claims, claims for sex and race discrimination, equal pay, accrued debts owed to the employee and other tortious liability (e.g., personal injury), will pass to the buyer under TUPE. It is therefore critical that the buyer obtains appropriate indemnities from the seller in respect of all pre-transfer liabilities.

Pension Rights

The major exceptions to the principle of automatic transfer are old age, invalidity and survivors' benefits under occupational pension schemes. These do not transfer under TUPE. However:

- An obligation in an employment contract to pay a percentage of salary into the employee's personal pension scheme will not fall within the exemption and therefore will be covered by the automatic transfer principle.
- Buyers must meet specified levels of pension provision for certain transferring employees.
- The exclusion does not apply to other benefits under an occupational pension scheme which are not old age, invalidity or survivors' benefits. This includes any early retirement benefits, including the right to retire early voluntarily.

Profit Share and Share Option Schemes

Certain categories of profit share and share option schemes by their nature may not be transferable. For example, on a transfer, employees might cease to be entitled to participate in the seller's group employee share option scheme. Indeed, some share option schemes provide that any options become exercisable on a TUPE transfer. In practice, it is not possible for a buyer to provide that the transferred employees will remain in the seller's share option scheme after they leave the seller's group of companies. Therefore, the buyer may be obligated to provide an equivalent share option scheme, even if it is a 'phantom' scheme. Alternatively, it may have to buy out those employees' rights.

Similar issues arise in relation to benefits that can only be provided by the seller (e.g., staff discounts).

Restrictive Covenants

Restrictive covenants also transfer with the rest of the contract, but the restrictive covenants will be interpreted and construed as at the time the contract was entered into. Therefore when, for example, identifying the range of activities or customers to which the post-termination restrictions apply, these will relate to those of the seller's business, not the buyer's. Depending on the particular circumstances of the case, it may be necessary for the buyer to arrange for the restrictive covenants to be amended, but this will be subject to the buyer's limited rights to make changes to the contract.

7.3. Acquisition Checklist

As part of its due diligence process, the buyer will want to obtain as much information as possible about the employees it will acquire, which may include details of the following:

- Employees and consultants working in the business, including the terms of their contract, wage agreements and recent pay awards, share option schemes, profit-related pay, pensions, cars, other benefits and personnel policies and details of any collective recognition and consultation arrangements, including any information and consultation agreements.
- Employees who will transfer under TUPE and anyone else who works in the business but who will not transfer under TUPE (e.g., consultants and employees who provide central administrative services on a group basis).
- Employees who are 'key' to the business. What is their notice period and are there any restrictive covenants that are applicable to them? What is their likely response to the sale? How important is it to retain them after the acquisition? Can they be replaced?
- Service agreements of the management team and details of their remuneration, salaries, notice periods and restrictive covenants.
- Contractual benefits, policies and insurances. Identify those that cannot, by their nature, be transferred (e.g., profit share schemes based on the seller's profits). Identify which schemes provided by third parties can be assigned to the buyer and take the necessary steps to assign them.

- Employees who have given or received notice and are currently working out their notice periods and details of those whose employment with the business will soon terminate.
- The number, location and functions of employees. Will additional employees be required? If redundancies may be necessary, how much will they cost? Are there any information and consultation requirements?
- Identify existing and potential employment claims, for example, for breach of contract, unfair dismissal or discrimination.
- Employee morale, turnover, training and competitiveness of employment terms.
- Particulars of labour relations, union recognition, strike experience and other disturbances and agreements or arrangements with unions or other worker representatives.

Both parties to a sale need to ensure that as much employee information as possible is anonymized in order to avoid breaching the Data Protection Act 1998 (DPA).

7.4. Sale of a Business

Where TUPE applies to the sale of a business, the seller and buyer have an obligation to inform and (if appropriate) consult with recognized trade unions or elected employee representatives in relation to any affected employees.

The seller is also required to provide certain employee liability information (ELI) to the buyer before the transfer (see below).

Affected Employees

The obligation to inform and consult is in relation to any 'affected' employees, defined as 'any employees of the transferor or the transferee who may be affected by the transfer or may be affected by measures taken in connection with it', including:

- employees who are to be transferred;
- employees of the seller who are not being transferred to the buyer but whose jobs may be affected by the transfer;
- employees of the buyer whose jobs may be affected as a result of the transfer.

Appropriate Representatives

Where an employer recognizes a trade union, it must inform and consult representatives of that union. The employer is not required to inform and consult any other employee representatives in such circumstances but may do so if the trade union is recognized for one group but not for another. Where no trade union is recognized, the employer must inform and consult either existing employee representatives or new ones specially elected for the purposes of the transfer. If they are to be existing representatives, their remit and appointment must give them suitable authority.

Obligation to Inform

The recognized trade union or elected employee representatives must be informed about the transfer (and any measures) long enough before the relevant transfer to enable consultations to take place. There is no minimum prescribed time limit, and much depends on the extent of any changes which are likely to take place.

What Information Is to Be Given?

TUPE provides that the following information must be given to the relevant recognized trade union or employee representatives:

- The fact of the transfer, the date (approximately, if necessary) when it is to take place and the reasons for it.
- The legal, economic and social implications of the transfer for the affected employees. What is meant by 'legal, economic and social implications' will be a question of fact in each case.
- The measures the employer envisages it will take in connection with the transfer in relation to 'any affected employees' or, if no measures are to be taken, that fact. The term 'measures' includes any 'action, step or arrangement' taken in connection with the transfer.
- The seller must also provide information about any measures the buyer envisages it will take in relation to the transferring employees in connection with the transfer or, if the buyer envisages taking no measures, that fact.

In relation to this last category of information, the buyer has an obligation to provide the information to the seller in time to allow the seller to perform its obligation to give the information to the union/employee representatives.

The seller and buyer are jointly and severally liable in relation to a failure to inform and consult under TUPE.

7.5 Sale Checklist

TUPE requires a seller in an asset purchase to provide the buyer with certain information about the transferring employees, known as the ELI. The ELI consists of:

- the identity and age of the employees who will transfer;
- information contained in those employees' written particulars of employment under section 1 ERA 1996;

- information on any collective agreements affecting those employees which will still have effect after the transfer;
- any disciplinary proceedings taken against an employee or grievance brought by an employee in the previous two years;
- any legal actions taken by those employees against the seller in the previous two years, and any such potential legal actions where the seller has reasonable grounds to believe such actions might occur.

8. USE OF ALTERNATIVE WORKFORCES: INDEPENDENT CONTRACTORS, CONTRACT EMPLOYEES, AND TEMPORARY OR LEASED WORKERS

8.1. Overview

Many types of atypical working patterns do not fit the classic or traditional concept of an employee working full-time for a single employer under a contract of service of indefinite length. There has been a rapid increase in flexibility and diversity of legal and economic relationships and practices in the workplace. This has made it harder to decide whether an individual, doing paid work, does so under an employment contract and, if so, for whom.

The employment status of an individual is important for a number of reasons. For example, certain important legal rights only apply if an individual is an employee. However, increasingly rights are also additionally being granted to other types of 'atypical' workers.

8.2. Independent Contractors

8.2.1. Definition

The term 'independent contractor' is commonly used to describe someone who is truly self-employed. The question of whether a person is an employee or self-employed is, for most purposes, determined by reference to the contract under which they work.

Under section 230(1) ERA 1996, an employee is defined as 'an individual who has entered into or works under (or, where the employment has ceased, worked under) a contract of employment'. Under section 230(2) ERA 1996, a contract of employment means 'a contract of service or apprenticeship, whether express or implied, and (if it is express) whether oral or in writing'.

The terms 'contract of service' and 'contract for services' have no statutory definition and the category into which a particular contract falls is determined according to case law. Generally, under a contract of service, a person agrees to serve another, whereas under a contract for services, they agree to provide certain services to that other.

Over the years, several different tests have been used to identify whether a contract is a contract of service or a contract for services. However, three areas have attracted the greatest degree of case law attention and been viewed as the central factors in determining whether an employment relationship exists. These are:

- *Personal service:* An employee would, other than in extremely limited and exceptional circumstances, be required to provide personal service, whereas it would be consistent with self-employed or independent contractor status to be able to provide a substitute or to subcontract the service obligations.
- *Mutuality of obligation:* This is the obligation on the employer to provide work and the obligation on the individual to accept that work. The significance of mutuality of obligation is that it determines whether there is a contract in existence at all, that is, if there is an obligation to provide work and a corresponding obligation on the individual to do the work that is offered, then there is mutuality of obligation. By contrast, with a self-employed individual, a company does not have to offer work, and when it is offered, the self-employed person may refuse the offer in favour of work from someone else – or simply because he does not want it.
- *Control:* In principle, an employee would normally be subject to control or supervision by the employer. There are several ways in which control is exhibited. One is the overall control over the contractual relationship, that is the power to terminate and, in particular, to subject the employee to disciplinary procedures and otherwise to manage the relationship by issuing orders and directions. A self-employed individual or an independent contractor would usually have a greater degree of freedom in their method of working than an employee. For example, they typically:
  (a) work more independently from the employer and are less likely to be subject to the same controls or supervision that would be exercised over an employee;
  (b) provide and maintain their own equipment; and
  (c) determine their own working days and hours.

Personal service, mutuality and control have been referred to as 'the irreducible minimum', which means that if any one of the three core areas is not established, there can be no contract of employment. It would, however, be bold to describe that as an incontrovertible rule and recent case law on these three areas provides support to that view, contributing little to the clarity of the situation.

However, there are other factors that are relevant to the question of whether someone is employed or self-employed. These factors include:

- Integration into business: The degree of integration into the employer's business could mean anything from being subject to the employer's disciplinary and grievance rules, to holding the employer's business cards, being given a job title within the organization and being invited to staff social events.

- Other activities An employee may well be restricted from working for others as employers expect exclusive service. Therefore, if the individual is free to provide services to others, and in fact does so, that may be a sign of self-employment.
- Description applied by the parties: How the parties describe themselves will never be the decisive factor but particularly in marginal cases, could be relevant.
- Nature and length of engagement: The nature of the engagement and its length may be relevant. A person engaged on an indeterminate basis might be more likely to appear to be an employee than someone taken on for a specific task, where the engagement lasts as long as the task does. The former situation often brings with it greater control, through the ability to reallocate the person to other tasks. Similarly, it is sometimes suggested that long periods working for one organization may be more likely to signal an employment relationship, although this may be for no better reason than that the longer the relationship continues the more likelihood there is of it being tested, especially if it exceeds one year (at which point the potential to claim unfair dismissal arises).
- Benefits and insurance: Generally speaking, the inclusion of a person in benefit schemes operated by the employer, such as share option schemes, health insurance and bonus schemes, will tend to indicate employment under a contract of service as it may signal greater integration and permanence. It could indeed be the case that the benefits are only open to employees (under the relevant scheme rules or the terms of the relevant insurance policies), so employment would in fact be a necessity.

Other factors could include:

- who provides work equipment;
- whether the person hires their own help;
- the degree of risk adopted;
- the degree of responsibility for investment and management;
- how far the individual profits from sound management; and
- the number of people by whom the individual is engaged.

8.2.2. Creating the Relationship

A written contract alone is not determinative of the status of a worker (i.e., whether someone is a genuine independent contractor) but it is an important factor the courts will take into account if status becomes an issue.

There is no requirement for a written contract (commonly referred to as a contract for services) between an independent contractor and another party but it is clearly advisable that all of the terms of the contract are written into one single document.

8.2.3. Compensation

Terms relating to how much the independent contractor is to be paid in return for providing his/her services are governed by the contract. Assuming an individual is a genuine independent contractor, the legislation applicable to employees has no relevance. However, if the independent contractor is also deemed a 'worker' there are some regulations which provide certain rights, such as a right to paid holiday. A worker, for these purposes, is defined as an individual who has entered into or works under:

- a contract of employment; or
- any other contract, whether express or implied and (if it is express) whether oral or in writing, whereby the individual undertakes to do or perform personally any work or services for another party to the contract whose status is not, by virtue of the contract, that of a client or customer of any profession or business undertaking carried on by the individual.

Depending on the circumstances, therefore, a worker can be an employee or someone working under a contract for services, where the individual provides the services personally for the other party.

8.2.4. Other Terms and Conditions

A contract for services is, in effect, a commercial agreement which may contain many of the terms and conditions that one sees in a contract of employment between two parties. However, in a contract for services, one would expect to see the following matters addressed:

- a description of the services to be provided by the independent contractor;
- whether the services can be subcontracted;
- a warranty that the independent contractor has appropriate insurances;
- notice to terminate provisions;
- confidentiality;
- an indemnity in favour of the other contracting party in the event that the HM Revenue and Customs deems the independent contractor to be an employee, and the other party is ordered to pay employment taxes (retroactive to the start of the contract);

A statement that both parties view the contractor as an 'independent contractor'.

8.3. CONTRACT WORKERS

Definition

Contract workers are often referred to as 'agency workers' because they are supplied by a third party or 'recruitment agency'.

Agency workers are often used:

- to cover for staff shortages caused by illness, holidays, sabbaticals or maternity leave;
- in industries, such as construction, to meet fluctuating demands; or
- to provide cover in unforeseen circumstances, for example, care givers, nannies and clerical staff.

A common issue for agency workers is whether they are employees of either the employment agency or of its client.

An employment relationship will only be found to exist between an agency worker and a client (also referred to as an 'end user') where it is necessary to give effect to the reality of the relationship (i.e., where it is in every respect an employer/employee relationship in all but name) to imply a contract of employment between them. In considering whether it is necessary to imply a contract of employment, employment tribunals will look at all the circumstances of a case: the documents that purport to record the arrangements between the parties as well as the reality of the situation, in particular the issues of mutuality of obligation and control.

The Agency Workers Regulations (AWR) 2010 came into effect on 1 October 2011 and apply to agency workers who are assigned to do temporary work (for hirers) through temporary work agencies. The AWR provide that all agency workers must be able to access a hirer's collective facilities and amenities and have access to information about its job vacancies from the first day of their assignment. In addition, after completion of a twelve-week qualifying period, agency workers are entitled to the same basic working and employment conditions.

No Obligation to Provide Salary, Wages and Benefits

An end user would not normally pay the agency worker directly; it is more common to pay the agency and the agency pays the employee.

No Right to Continued Work

The benefit of using agency workers is that an end user can stop using them with little or no notice, depending on their terms with the agency.

Laws are due to be introduced in the future which will provide agency workers with more protection and rights than they currently have.

8.4. Leased Workers

The same provisions above apply to leased workers, that is, workers supplied to a company for a longer period of time.

8.5. Checklist of Do's and Don'ts

- Ensure that a written contract is drafted which clearly defines the relationship between the parties and ensure that it is consistent with independent contractor (and not employee) status.
- Consider the nature of the services to be provided by an independent contractor and assess whether the person providing the services is truly an independent contractor.
- Focus on using independent contractors for specific projects or to cover for fixed periods.
- For those independent contractors providing their services on a regular basis, build in a review of their status, which can change over time, at three or six monthly intervals.
- Avoid using independent contractors continuously for lengthy periods, certainly over a year, unless it is clear that they are working on a specific contract.

Minimize any integration into the workforce. Avoid giving independent contractors management or supervisory roles, training them or involving them in employee events such as employee briefings, team-building exercises and company social events.

- If using an agency to provide contract workers, use an agency that is organized, that properly documents its relationships with workers and clients (and appreciates the potential for the implications of employment contracts). Comply with the Agency Workers Regulations.
- On a day-to-day basis, reduce control of independent contractors or agency contracted workers and avoid appraising or disciplining them.
- Pass dealings with agency workers through the agency.
- Seek an indemnity from the independent contractor or the agency (in the case of agency workers) in respect of claims based on employment status and potential claims by HM Revenue and Customs for 'employee' taxes.
- Request that the independent contractor provide the services via his/her own service company (this may help the company avoid liability for tax but won't necessarily avoid statutory employment claims).

9. OBLIGATION TO BARGAIN COLLECTIVELY WITH TRADE UNIONS: EMPLOYEES' RIGHT TO STRIKE AND A COMPANY'S RIGHT TO CONTINUE BUSINESS OPERATIONS

9.1. Overview of Unions' Rights to Organize

A trade union is an organization made up of members (a membership-based organization) and its membership must be made up mainly of workers. One of a trade union's main aims is to protect and advance the interests of its members in the workplace.

Most trade unions are independent of any employer. However, trade unions try to develop close working relationships with employers. This can sometimes take the form of a partnership agreement between the employer and the trade union which identifies their common interests and objectives.

Trade unions:

- negotiate agreements with employers on pay and conditions;
- discuss major changes to the workplace such as large-scale redundancy;
- discuss their members' concerns with employers;
- accompany their members in disciplinary and grievance meetings;
- provide their members with legal and financial advice;
- provide education facilities and certain consumer benefits such as discounted insurance.

9.2. Right of Employees to Join Unions

Employees may join an independent trade union. Those who do so, benefit from certain bargaining rights if their union is recognized by their employer.

9.3. How Employees Select Unions

An independent trade union that wishes to be recognized to conduct collective bargaining on behalf of a group of workers (referred to as the 'bargaining unit') will need to be recognized by the employer.

Usually recognition is sought by negotiation with the employer. However, if agreement cannot be reached, provided that the employer has at least twenty-one employees, the union may seek statutory recognition by following the statutory procedure set out in the Trade Union and Labour Relations (Consolidation) Act 1992 (TULRCA).

The union makes a written request for recognition directly to the employer. If the employer rejects the offer, the union must submit an application for recognition to the Central Arbitration Committee (CAC).

Once a union has started the statutory recognition process, the employer and union may agree that the union should be recognized to conduct collective bargaining on behalf of a group of workers employed by the employer. This is referred to by the CAC as 'semi-voluntary recognition'. Otherwise, once the CAC has received an application for recognition from a union, the main issues that the CAC will decide are:

- Whether the application is admissible and can be accepted. The CAC must be satisfied that at least 10% of the workers in the union's proposed bargaining unit are members of the union and that a majority of workers within the bargaining unit are likely to support recognition of the union.
- If the application is accepted, whether the bargaining unit proposed by the union is appropriate, determined primarily by the size of the group of employees that forms the bargaining unit, and if it is not, what the bargaining unit should be. If a bargaining unit changes after the CAC has accepted an application (either as the result of agreement between the parties or a decision by the CAC), the CAC must decide whether the application can continue.
- Once an appropriate bargaining unit has been agreed or decided, the level of support for the union in the bargaining unit. If the CAC is not satisfied that a majority of workers in the bargaining unit are members of the union it will arrange for the employees in the bargaining unit to hold a secret ballot to be held regarding the support for recognition of the union. It may order a ballot in any event.
- What the method of collective bargaining should be if, once a union is recognized, the union and employer are unable to agree a method between themselves.

Once the CAC has accepted a union's application for recognition in respect of a particular bargaining unit, no matter what the outcome, no further application can be accepted from that union in respect of that bargaining unit, or a substantially similar bargaining unit, for another three years.

The term 'accepted' relates to a preliminary hurdle which needs to be overcome before the CAC will consider the application.

The CAC needs to be satisfied of the following before accepting an application:

- The union has made an application for recognition to the employer.
- The application accurately reflects the position reached between the parties.
- The application is admissible.[4]

4. Paragraph 15(2), Sch. A1, TULRCA.

In order for an application to be admissible:

- the application must be made using the CAC's application form;
- the union must give notice of the application, a copy of the application and of any documents supporting it to the employer; and
- the CAC must be satisfied that:
  - (a) at least 10% of the workers in the bargaining unit are members of the union; and
  - (b) a majority of workers in the bargaining unit would be likely to be in favour of the union conducting collective bargaining on their behalf.

9.4. Pre-election Campaigning

The Secretary of State has published a Code of Practice called 'Access and Unfair Practices during Recognition and Derecognition Ballots' (the AURD Code). Although the AURD Code does not impose legal obligations (a failure to observe it will not, of itself, give rise to proceedings) that is, legal claims in the courts and liability, it is admissible in evidence and must be taken into account in any proceedings before a court, tribunal or the CAC if they consider it relevant.

The AURD Code makes several recommendations for providing unions with access to the workers in a bargaining unit, including making arrangements for the union to have access (including entering an access agreement) and determining who should have access to the workers in a bargaining unit, at what times and in what places.

The AURD Code addresses several issues that the parties should consider at the outset of being notified that a ballot is to be held:

- The union should request a meeting with the employer to discuss ballot arrangements. The employer should agree to arrange the meeting at a mutually convenient time on an early date.
- The employer and union should ensure that their representatives at the meeting are expressly authorized to take all relevant decisions regarding access, or are authorized to make recommendations directly to those who make such decisions.
- When a ballot concerns a joint application for recognition by two or more unions, the unions should act jointly in preparing and implementing access arrangements (unless the employer and unions agree otherwise).
- The union will need to reveal its plans for on-site access to the employer. The employer should accept them unless it considers them unreasonable. Alternatives should be offered at the earliest opportunity to replace rejected proposals (preferably within three working days of receipt of the union's initial proposals).
- It is reasonable for the union to request information from the employer to help it formulate and refine its access proposals. The employer should give

the union information about the typical methods it uses to communicate with its workforce and other practical information (whether about premises or patterns of work) that may assist the union to develop an access proposal.
- The employer should not disclose to the union the names or addresses (postal or e-mail) of the workers who will be balloted, unless the workers concerned have authorized such disclosure.
- Where relevant, the employer should also tell the union about its own plans for putting its views across to its workers.
- It would be reasonable, particularly given potential security and health and safety issues, for an employer to want to give prior permission before a full-time union officer comes on site to talk to its workers.

The AURD Code recommends that, where possible, parties should consider entering a written agreement on access arrangements. This should include:

- the union's programme for where, when and how it will access the workers on site and during their working time, as well as a mechanism for resolving disagreements about implementing those arrangements; and
- any understanding that has been reached about the standards of conduct expected of the parties and those who campaign on their behalf.

To avoid misunderstanding, the employer should ensure that relevant managers (and the union should ensure that relevant officials and representatives) are aware of the access agreement/arrangements and the commitments the employer has undertaken to release workers to attend access meetings.

If circumstances require the amendment of an access agreement, the union or employer should notify the other of required changes at the earliest opportunity and suggest alternatives. Alternatives that are equivalent to those they replace should generally be agreed.

Where the employer and the union fail to agree on access arrangements, the following may result:

- Either party may ask ACAS to conciliate. ACAS will respond to the conciliation request as soon as possible, preferably within one working day of receiving the request.
- If matters remain deadlocked, the CAC may be asked to assist. The CAC can consider delaying the ballot for a limited period to give the parties extra time to settle their differences. It can also be asked to adjudicate and make an order.

An access agreement should specify who will have access to the workers being balloted. Employers should be prepared to give access to the following:

- Individual union members it employs who are nominated as the union's lead representative at a workplace where the bargaining unit is located and, provided it is practicable for them to attend, lead representatives from other

workplaces in the employer's business. The union and individuals should share the costs of travelling between workplaces.
- Full-time union officials (those employed by the union who are officials within the meaning of sections 1 and 19 of TULRCA 1992).

The number of union representatives entitled to access should be proportionate to the scale and nature of the activities or events taking place during the agreed access programme.

The AURD Code recommends that, where practicable, access should be at the workers' workplace. However:

- Each case will depend on the type of workplace and the union will need to take account of physical arrangements and operational requirements (in particular, those relating to security or health and safety).
- Where appropriate, the employer's typical methods of communicating with its workforce should be used as a benchmark for deciding how the union should communicate with that workforce during the access period. For example, if the employer usually holds large meetings in a canteen or meeting room, these facilities should be offered to the union.
- Exceptionally, due to the nature of the employer's business or severe space limitations, access may need to be restricted to meetings away from the workplace. The employer should give the union reasonable assistance to notify workers of the time and location of off-site meetings.

The AURD Code suggests that a union's access to the workforce should be guided by the employer's usual arrangements for communicating with its workforce. Access should:

- usually be during normal working hours but at times which minimize disruption to the employer's activities, for example, during rest periods or towards the end of a shift;
- where required by exceptional circumstances, take place at a meeting arranged away from the workplace. If the venue is within easy walking distance the meeting can be held during work time. Otherwise, it should be held outside work time.

The AURD Code recommends that the parties should agree to limits on the duration and frequency of the union's activities during the access period:

- The union should be allowed to hold one meeting of at least thirty minutes duration for every ten days of the access period, which all workers or a substantial proportion of them have the opportunity to attend.
- In total, the union should have the same number of large-scale meetings as the employer during the access period.

It also suggests that union 'surgeries' could be organized during working hours at the workplace so that workers can meet a union representative for fifteen minutes on an individual basis or in groups of two or three. However:

- whether surgeries are appropriate would depend on demand, whether they could be arranged off-site as effectively, whether they would cause tension at the workplace and whether the employer uses similar one-on-one or small meetings to advance its case; if surgeries do not take place, the minimum time for each large-scale meeting should be forty-five minutes;
- workers conducting and attending surgeries should be paid in full for the duration of their absence from work (but not where attendance is at a time when they would not normally be receiving pay);
- the employer should be given as much notice as possible of surgeries and exceptionally (where there is not adequate cover or the provision of a service could not otherwise be maintained) may refuse time off.

9.5. Unfair Labour Practices

The AURD Code notes that active campaigning needs to be responsible or it can lead to the use of unfair practices which distort the balloting process, increase workplace friction and negatively impact employment relations.

Examples of unfair practices include the following:

- An offer, by either union or employer, to pay each worker GBP 100, if the ballot does (or does not) result in recognition.
- An offer of 'money's worth' includes non-cash offers (usually the provision of goods and services which workers would otherwise have to pay for, such as a better company car, subsidized health insurance, free legal services, additional holiday pay or other paid leave).
- Offering money's worth for permissible reasons (e.g., a normal inducement to join a union or as a typical bonus for meeting a work target) is not an unfair practice.
- Disciplinary action taken by the employer to influence the results of the ballot (whether against a worker entitled to vote in the ballot or another worker, such as a union activist involved in the union's campaign).

Undue influence covers a wide range of behaviour from the obvious, such as threats of physical violence, to the more subtle, such as the offer of better pay or conditions during the ballot period (unless that is the normal time for a pay review or there is a pressing reason, unconnected with the ballot, for doing so).

9.6. Relocation of Work/Shutdown of Business

Employers have a duty to consult Trade Unions when they propose to dismiss as redundant twenty or more employees at one establishment within a period of ninety days or less. See section 6.2 above.

9.7. Checklist of Do's and Don'ts

- Try to reach a negotiated agreement on the recognition of a Trade Union rather than having a system imposed by the CAC.
- Do not give personal details about employees to Trade Unions for the purpose of arranging a ballot, unless the employees have consented.
- Consider arrangements dealing with access to employees and ensure that such arrangements are written down.
- Do not attempt to influence the outcome of a ballot with the use of unfair practices.

10. WORKING CONDITIONS: HOURS OF WORK AND PAYMENT OF WAGES: BY STATUTE OR COLLECTIVE AGREEMENTS

10.1. Overview of Wage and Hour Laws

Laws in relation to wages and hours of work are provided in the ERA 1996 and the WTR 1998.

Until the introduction of the WTR, hours of work were largely unregulated, although there had earlier been specific rules in force relating to the employment of women (since repealed), and rules concerning the employment of children and young people, which remained. The WTR introduced, for the first time, rules of general application (albeit with certain exceptions) limiting working hours and providing for rest breaks and holidays.

10.2. Minimum Wage

The national minimum wage (NMW) was introduced in 1999 by the National Minimum Wage Act 1998 (NMWA 1998). It gives workers the right to a specified minimum hourly rate of pay, which is regularly updated. The employer is under the obligation to pay the NMW, and there are no exclusions for smaller employers.

The provisions relating to the NMW are contained in the NMWA 1998 and in the National Minimum Wage Regulations 1999 (the NMW Regulations).

The NMWA 1998 provides for different rates of NMW for three different categories of workers, namely:

- *Standard (adult) rate*: workers aged 22 or over (there is no upper age limit);
- *Development rate*: workers aged between 18 and 21 inclusive;
- *Young workers rate*: workers aged under 18 but over 16 (the compulsory school age) that are not apprentices.

The National Living Wage is an obligatory minimum wage payable to workers in the United Kingdom aged over 25 which came into effect on 1 April 2016. As of April 2018, it is GBP 7.83 per hour for those aged 25 and over, GBP 7.38 for those aged 21–24, GBP 5.90 for ages 18–20 and GBP 5.90 for under 18.

10.3. Overtime

The WTR imposes a restriction on the maximum number of hours that can be worked each week. A worker's average working time (including all overtime) must not exceed forty-eight hours per week. An employer must take all reasonable steps, in keeping with the need to protect health and safety, to ensure that this limit is complied with. Failure to do so is an offence punishable with a potentially unlimited fine.

The limit on average working hours does not apply if the employer has 'obtained the worker's agreement in writing' to perform work in excess of the limit. This is generally referred to as an 'opt-out agreement'. The opt-out agreement can last for a fixed period or indefinitely. Any opted-out worker can cancel the opt-out by giving at least seven days', notice unless the opt-out agreement provides for longer notice, which cannot exceed three months.

The following points should be considered with regard to 'opt-outs':

- Even if a worker has agreed to opt-out of the limits, he cannot be required to work excessively long hours if this creates a reasonably foreseeable risk to his own health and safety or the health and safety of others, since the employer has a duty at common law to protect workers' health and safety.
- Employers must keep records covering the last two years showing which workers have opted out.
- The opt-out should specify that the worker agrees to disapply the statutory forty-eight-hour limit and not simply state that they agree to work more than forty-eight hours. Further, in order to override any existing contractual provisions limiting hours of work, the opt-out agreement must be sufficiently certain to constitute a variation of the existing contract, and should therefore specify the new working hours.

- Employers pressuring workers to sign an opt-out or victimizing anyone for refusing to do so, risk infringing the provisions of section 45A ERA 1996. An employer can refuse to accept an employee's request to opt-out, but must be consistent in doing so to avoid potential discrimination or victimization claims.
- Although it is unlawful to dismiss a worker or otherwise victimize them for refusing to sign an opt-out or for opting back in, there is currently no prohibition on refusing to employ someone unless they opt-out. Some employers include an opt-out in job offer letters or in the contract of employment itself, but this practice has attracted considerable criticism from both unions and employers as being an abuse of the opt-out.
- Subject to the NMW, rates of pay for hours of work and overtime are a matter of contract between the parties.

10.4. Meal and Rest Periods

A worker is entitled to daily rest of eleven uninterrupted hours in every twenty-four-hour period and weekly rest of twenty-four uninterrupted hours in every seven-day period. At the employer's choice, the weekly rest period can consist of two uninterrupted twenty-four-hour rests or one uninterrupted forty-eight-hour rest in every fourteen-day period. There is no need to formally record this choice or even to communicate it to the workers, although thought should be given to which approach is to be taken and to maintaining consistency. The employer can adopt differing approaches for different grades of worker or different locations.

The weekly rest period should not include any part of a daily rest period unless this is justified by objective or technical reasons, or reasons concerning the organization of work. In other words, the daily and weekly rest entitlements are cumulative, meaning that a worker should typically have 35 hours' continuous rest (24+11) once a week. Alternatively, if the employer chooses to provide 48 hours' rest every two weeks, the worker is entitled to have 11 hours' daily rest for twelve days, followed by one continuous rest period of 59 hours rest (48+11) every two weeks.

For the purposes of weekly rest, the seven-day or fourteen-day period begin at the start of a week, which, in the absence of contrary agreement, starts at midnight between Sunday and Monday. Any relevant agreement (i.e., an individual, collective or workforce agreement in writing) can be used to vary this.

Workers can still elect to work additional hours by foregoing their rest entitlements under the WTR, provided the employer does not breach the forty-eight-hour average (averaged over seventeen weeks) weekly limit or the rules on night working, and provided there is no additional foreseeable risk to health and safety. If this is the employee's choice, there is no statutory requirement to provide compensatory rest for forgone rest breaks.

Workers have the right to take an uninterrupted twenty-minute rest break, away from the workstation, if their day's working time is more than six hours. Workers can be required to remain in or about their workplace (but not at their workstation) while taking a rest break, provided that they are not still required to perform any duties. However, there is no need under the WTR, for employers to provide separate facilities or accommodation for workers to take a rest break.

The break need not be paid. In many cases the obligation to provide a rest break is already satisfied by the provision of meal breaks. There is no restriction as to when the break must be taken but it should ideally be taken near the middle of the shift.

Note that the right is limited to twenty minutes break per day and so during a twelve-hour shift (for example), only one break need be offered (subject to the employer's general duty to prevent risks to health and safety).

Employers may use a collective or workforce agreement to exclude or modify the right to the rest break provided compensatory rest is given wherever possible. A collective or workforce agreement may also be used to determine the duration of the rest break or the terms on which it is granted. For example, the agreement may allow the employer to split the break into two or more shorter periods but, in return, the workers' representatives may seek a greater overall length of breaks, or may seek to agree that the breaks be paid.

It must be clear to workers, when they start a rest break, that that is what they are doing. A period of 'downtime' cannot retrospectively become a rest break just because it turns out to have lasted at least twenty minutes.

10.5. Deductions from Wages

The ERA 1996 sets out the provisions that protect workers from unauthorized deductions being made from their wages.

The basic position under section 13 ERA 1996 is that it is unlawful to make a deduction from a worker's wages unless:

- the deduction is required or authorized by statute or a provision in the worker's contract; or
- the worker has given their prior written consent to the deduction.

An employer can lawfully make a deduction from a worker's wages if the payment is required or authorized by statute. This includes:

- deductions for income tax and national insurance contributions under the pay (tax) as you earn (PAYE) system; and
- deductions made pursuant to the Attachment of Earnings Act 1971 (which enables the courts to make attachment of earnings orders).

If the deduction is made under a provision of the worker's contract, then the worker must have seen the term or (if it is not a written contract) must have been told in writing of its effect before the deduction is made.

The contractual provision and the worker's prior written consent need to make it clear that the deduction will be made from the worker's wages. The employer must also demonstrate that the event justifying the deduction has occurred.

There are a number of express exceptions to the basic position outlined above. If a deduction falls within these exceptions it will be outside the scope of the ERA 1996 and, accordingly, outside the employment tribunal's jurisdiction.

The specific exceptions are set out in section 14 ERA 1996:

- Deductions made in order to reimburse the employer in respect of an overpayment of wages or an overpayment in relation to expenses incurred by the worker in carrying out their employment.
- Deductions made in connection with any disciplinary proceedings held by virtue of a statutory provision.
- Deductions made in accordance with a statutory requirement to deduct and pay over to a public authority amounts determined by that authority to be due to it from the worker, such as HM Revenue and Customs.
- Deductions payable to third parties (e.g., employees' contributions to a pension scheme or trade union dues) made either pursuant to a contractual term (to which the worker has agreed in writing) or otherwise with their prior written agreement or consent.
- Deductions made from a worker's wages for taking part in a strike or other industrial action.
- Deductions made to satisfy an order of a court or tribunal for the payment of an amount by the worker to the employer, provided the worker has given their prior written consent.

10.6. Garnishment

An attachment of earnings order is an order that compels a judgment debtor's employer to make regular deductions from the debtor's earnings and pay them to the Court. An application for an attachment of earnings order will only be successful if all the following conditions are met:

- The judgment debtor is behind with at least one payment towards the judgment debt.
- The amount remaining due under the judgment is at least GBP 50.
- The debtor is employed (an order cannot be made if the debtor is self-employed or unemployed).
- The debtor is not (a) a firm or company; or (b) in the armed forces, or (c) a merchant seaman.
- It is made within six years of the judgment.

10.7. Exemptions to Wage and Hour Laws

Certain sectors are excluded from the provisions of the WTR with regard to hours or rest breaks (or both), such as rail workers, mobile workers, junior doctors, etc. Separate regulations have been enacted to deal with the very specific nature of the work done in these sectors. Employers need to consider carefully the extent of exemptions and any other regulations which are relevant to the specific sector.

10.8. Child Labour

The Children and Young Persons Act (CYPA) 1933 sets out minimum age requirements, restrictions on the hours that children can work and the type of work in which they can be involved. In addition to the restrictions set out in the CYPA, a child's absence from school due to employment, whether paid or unpaid, would be treated as an unauthorized absence by a local education authority (LEA) and could lead to action being taken against the child's parents.

Age Limits

Children under 14 years old may not be employed. However, this rule can be and often is relaxed by local authority byelaws to allow 13-year-old children to be employed, for example, to deliver newspapers, to stack shelves, etc. Therefore, employers wishing to employ children aged 13 should contact the local authority where the employment is to take place to find out if the local authority has issued byelaws permitting employment of children of that age. Byelaws allowing children aged between 10 and 12 years old to be employed in light agricultural or horticultural work on an occasional basis, under parental supervision, have been unlawful since 2000.

Type of Work

Children can only be employed to do 'light work' defined as work that is unlikely to be harmful to the child's safety, health or development or to their school attendance. Furthermore, the CYPA states that a child cannot engage in or be employed in street trading. However, a local authority may make byelaws authorizing parents to employ their children aged 14 years and over in street trading. The byelaws:

- must contain provisions setting out the days and hours during which, and the places where, such children may be employed in street trading;
- may distinguish between ages and sexes of children and different localities;
- may regulate the conditions on which such licenses may be granted, suspended and revoked.

Hours of Work

Under the CYPA, children cannot be employed under the following conditions:

- On a school day, before the end of the school day. This rule is often relaxed by local authority byelaws to allow a child to do a newspaper round in the morning before school starts.
- Before 7 a.m. or after 7 p.m.
- For more than two hours on a day that they have to go to school or on a Sunday.
- For more than twelve hours in any school term week (a week being a period of seven consecutive days).
- For more than five hours on any non-school day from Monday to Saturday if they are under 15 years old. If they are 15 years old and over, for more than eight hours on a non-school day from Monday to Saturday.
- During school holidays, for more than twenty-five hours in the week if they are under 15 years old; or if they are 15 years old and over, for more than thirty-five hours in the week. This means that if the school term ends on a Tuesday, a 15-year-old child has to wait until the following Tuesday until they can work for thirty hours.
- Without a one hour rest break after working four hours in any day. It makes no difference if the child has already had a shorter break within that four-hour period.

Pay

There are no statutory restrictions on the rates of pay that can be offered to children. Children are not entitled to receive the NMW. However, young persons are entitled to receive the NMW at a 'young workers' rate.

Holidays

Children must be given a two-week break from any employment in each year. However, there is no statutory right to paid annual leave under the WTR 1998.

Rest Breaks

Subject to a few exceptions, young workers have greater entitlements to rest breaks than adult workers:

- Daily rest of twelve consecutive hours.
- A weekly rest period of forty-eight hours.
- A rest break of thirty minutes where daily working time is more than four and a half hours.

10.9. Recordkeeping Requirements

There are few statutory obligations on employers to collect and retain personal information about employees during employment. That said, for various reasons, employers collect and use information (personal data) in respect of employees at every stage of the employment relationship: when recruiting, while employing and even after the termination of employment:

- Information that Must Be Maintained
  Not applicable.
- Records that Must Be Retained
  Not applicable.
- Failure to Maintain Required Records
  Not applicable.

10.10. Reductions in Compensation Caused by Economic Downturn

An employer wishing to reduce an employee's salary or benefits would be acting in breach of contract unless there is a specific clause in the contract of employment permitting such reduction. A general clause allowing an employer the flexibility to change a contract of employment is unlikely to be sufficient. Even with a specific clause allowing such a change, it must be exercised reasonably if the employer is to avoid a successful claim of constructive unfair dismissal resulting from a resignation by the employee.

In practice, clauses allowing for a reduction in salary are not commonly seen in contracts. Therefore, if an employer wishes to reduce an employee's salary the only way this can be achieved, if a breach of contract is to be avoided, is to terminate the contract on notice and replace this with a new contract with the new terms relating to remuneration. This may of course still have consequences for the employer since the termination of contract would be a dismissal which the employee could challenge as unfair. An employer would only be able to avoid a successful claim of unfair dismissal in these circumstances if it can establish a sound business reason for the change to the contract, and it acted reasonably in introducing the change (i.e., fully consulted the employee).

A reduction in salary represents such a drastic change to the contract that an employer will need to provide compelling reasons why it needs to reduce an employee's salary if it wishes to avoid a successful claim of unfair dismissal.

10.11. Checklist of Do's and Don'ts

Ensure that a forty-eight-hour week opt-out agreement is freely signed by the employee. Preferably, the agreement should be separate to the contract of employment. If such an agreement is not signed, records will need to be kept of hours the employee worked.

Ensure that a clause is written into the contract of employment allowing for deductions from salary in particular circumstances, for example such as where an employee wishes to claw back training costs when his/her employment terminates before or shortly after training has completed.

Ensure that there is full compliance with the NMW.

11. OTHER WORKING CONDITIONS AND BENEFITS: BY STATUTE, COLLECTIVE AGREEMENTS, OR COMPANY POLICY

11.1. Health and Other Insurance

There is no obligation on an employer in England and Wales to provide health and other insurance benefits to employees.

11.2. Pension and Retirement Benefits

State Pensions

There are two types of pension provisions in the UK: state and private pensions. The state pension comprises two parts: the basic state pension and state second pension (S2P). Individuals are eligible to receive the basic state pension if they have paid sufficient national insurance contributions (NICs) during their working life. The basic state pension can be claimed from state pension age. The state pension age (which is set by law) is 65 years old for men and (currently) 60 years old for women (the state pension age for women will rise gradually from age 60 to 65 from 2010 to 2020). The state pension age will often be the same as an employee's contractual retirement age, or the normal retirement age under the employer's pension scheme but this is not always the case.

Until April 2002, the S2P was called the state earnings-related pension scheme (SERPS). This is also based on the NICs the individual has paid, however, it aims to provide a more generous additional state pension for low and moderate earners and certain care givers and long-term disabled people, by treating such people as having made the necessary minimum NICs. Individuals can choose to contract out of S2P by joining a contracted-out occupational pension scheme or taking out an appropriate personal pension scheme.

Auto-Enrolment

Employers in England and Wales are now required to provide employees with membership to a pension scheme. They can use an occupational pension scheme or personal pension scheme provided it meets certain statutory requirements. If they wish, they can enrol employees into a central scheme set up by the government. An employee can opt-out of either type of scheme once he has been automatically enrolled. But while he remains an active member, his employer will be required to pay a minimum level of pension contributions.

11.3. Vacation and Holiday Payments on Termination

On termination of employment, a worker is entitled to pay in lieu of unused annual leave. The amount of the payment is calculated in accordance with either a relevant agreement or, where there is no such agreement, the pay the worker would have received if he had taken a period of holiday.

11.4. Leaves of Absence

a. Personal Leave

There is no statutory right to take personal leave.

b. Medical or Sick Leave

Employees are permitted time off by their employer when they unable to attend work due to illness. Many employers do provide employees with normal pay for a limited number of days' sick leave each year but there is no obligation to do so. Employees may be entitled to statutory sick pay[5] for a fixed period of time, subject to certain qualifying conditions. Some employers provide employees with membership to a permanent health insurance plan, which will provide payment of salary (normally in the region of 75% of salary) where an employee is absent due to sickness for a period of three months or more.

c. Bereavement Leave

There is no statutory right to take bereavement leave. Such leave, and whether it is paid, is a matter to be determined by the employer.

5. As of 6 Apr. 2018 the weekly rate of SSP is GBP 92.05. It is reviewed and generally increased each year.

d. Family Leave

The concept of 'family leave' is not recognized in England and Wales. 'Family-Friendly' rights, however, include the following:

- *Dependent leave*: allows an employee to take a reasonable period of time off to care for a dependent.
- *Parental leave*: is a form of statutory unpaid leave available to some working parents in addition to statutory maternity, paternity and adoption leave. It can last up to thirteen weeks and can be flexible in terms of the time at which it is taken and the way in which the total leave entitlement may be split up into a number of shorter periods.

e. Pregnancy Leave

All pregnant employees have a statutory right to paid time off for antenatal care, regardless of hours worked or length of service. The employee is entitled to take reasonable time off during working hours. According to the Government's guidance, antenatal care is not restricted to medical examinations and could include relaxation classes and parentcraft classes, provided that these are advised by a registered medical practitioner, registered midwife or registered health visitor.

Expectant fathers do not have a legal right to time off to accompany their partners to antenatal appointments.

f. Maternity Leave

All pregnant employees, regardless of length of service, are entitled to fifty-two weeks of statutory maternity leave, consisting of twenty-six weeks' ordinary maternity leave (OML) and twenty-six weeks' additional maternity leave (AML).

If the employee satisfies minimum earnings criteria and has twenty-six weeks' continuous employment at the end of the fifteenth week before the Expected Week of Childbirth (EWC), she may be eligible for statutory maternity pay (SMP) for up to thirty-nine weeks.

SMP is payable at two different rates:

- First six weeks: the 'earnings-related rate' (90% of the employee's 'normal weekly earnings').
- Remaining thirty-three weeks: at a lower rate prescribed weekly rate of GBP 145.18.[6]

Since April 2015 a new system of shared parental leave and pay was introduced. Subject to certain conditions being met, the new system allows mothers and

6. Rate correct as of 6 Apr. 2018. It is reviewed, and generally increased, each year.

fathers to share the twelve-month period of maternity leave and entitlement to maternity pay between them.

g. Injury at Work

Time off due to injury at work is likely to be covered by an employer's normal rules on sickness absence.

11.5. Checklist of Do's and Don'ts

Set out in a relevant policy the circumstances when an employee is entitled to be paid for time taken off work.

If insurances are to be provided as a benefit, ensure that entitlement is always subject to the terms of the insurance scheme and ensure that flexibility is maintained to change the insurance provider and/or the scheme where necessary.

12. WORKERS' COMPENSATION

12.1. Overview

There is no equivalent to the US workers' compensation scheme in England and Wales.

12.2. Checklist of Do's and Don'ts

Not applicable.

13. COMPANY'S OBLIGATION TO PROVIDE SAFE AND HEALTHY WORKPLACE

13.1. Overview of Safety and Environmental Laws and Regulations

Employers have common law and statutory duties relating to the health and safety of their employees, contractors and members of the public.

At common law, employers:

- must provide and maintain a safe place of work, a safe system of work and safe plant and machinery;
- must employ competent staff;

- can be vicariously liable for the results of the negligent acts of their employees while working in the course of their employment;
- can be liable for certain occupational diseases (e.g., asbestosis) if they are considered to have been on notice of the risks of the disease materializing.

Under the Health and Safety at Work etc. Act 1974 (HSWA 1974), its related regulations and approved codes of practice:

- An employer has a general duty 'to ensure, so far as is reasonably practicable, the health, safety and welfare at work of all [its] employees'.
- In particular, an employer should ensure:
  - (a) provision and maintenance of plant and systems of work that are, so far as is reasonably practicable, safe and without risks to health;
  - (b) safe use, handling, storage and transport of articles and substances;
  - (c) information, instruction, training and supervision as is required to ensure, so far as is reasonably practicable, the health and safety of employees at work;
  - (d) places of work under the employer's control are, so far as is reasonably practicable, safe for work and without risks to health (with safe entrances and exits);
  - (e) provision and maintenance of a safe working environment with adequate facilities and arrangements for welfare at work.

13.2. Requirements

If an employer employs five or more people, it must have a written statement of its general health and safety policy (a health and safety policy statement) with respect to its employees and organization, and arrangements for carrying out the policy and bringing it to the attention of all its employees.

A written document ensures that both the employer and its workforce are clear about their respective responsibilities. Therefore, although an employer with less than five people in its workforce is not legally obliged to have a written health and safety policy statement, a written policy can improve health and safety within its organization.

Employees also have responsibilities under health and safety legislation, such as:

- to take reasonable care for their health and safety and that of anyone who may be affected by their acts or omissions while at work; and
- to cooperate with their employer so far as is necessary to enable compliance with any statutory duty or requirement relating to health and safety.

13.3. Rights of Employees

Generally, employees can expect the following with regard to health and safety at work:

- To work in places where all the risks to their health and safety are properly controlled.
- To stop working and leave the working area if they think they are in danger.
- To inform their employer about health and safety issues or concerns.
- To contact HSE or their local authority if they still have health and safety concerns.
- To join a trade union and be a safety representative.
- To paid time off work for training if they are a safety representative.

13.4. Rights of Employer

The employer has obligations, not rights, under health and safety law.

13.5. Specific Standards

The Management of Health and Safety at Work Regulations 1999 (the Management Regulations) generally make more explicit what employers are required to do to manage health and safety under the HSWA. Like the Act, they apply to every work activity. The main requirement on employers is to carry out a risk assessment. Employers with five or more employees need to record the significant findings of the risk assessment.

Risk assessments should be straightforward in a simple workplace such as a typical office. It should only be complicated if it deals with serious hazards such as those on a nuclear power station, a chemical plant, laboratory or an oil rig.

13.6. Injury or Accident at Work

An employer has a legal duty under the Reporting of Injuries, Diseases and Dangerous Occurrences Regulations 1995 to report the following types of incidents to the Health and Safety Executive:

- Deaths.
- Major injuries.
- Over-three-day injuries – where an employee or self-employed person is away from work or unable to perform their normal work duties for more than three consecutive days.

- Injuries to members of the public or people not at work where they are taken from the scene of an accident to the hospital.
- Some work-related diseases.
- Dangerous occurrences – where something happens that does not result in an injury, but could have done any injury.
- Gas Safe registered gas fitters must also report dangerous gas fittings they find, and gas conveyors/suppliers must report some flammable gas incidents.

Employers must keep a record of any reportable injury, disease or dangerous occurrence. This must include the date and method of reporting; the date, time and place of the event; personal details of those involved; and a brief description of the nature of the event or disease. Records can be kept in any of the following formats:

- Keeping paper copies of report forms in a file.
- Recording the details on a computer.
- Using an Accident Book system.
- Maintaining a written log.

13.7. Workplace Violence

An employer must provide a safe place of work. Violence at work would, in most cases, justify the dismissal of an offender.

13.8. Fines and Penalties

Health and safety inspectors can serve the following formal notices on employers without going to court:

- *Improvement notices*: These require the employer to remedy a fault or institute a programme of work within twenty-one days if, in the opinion of the inspector, the employer is (a) contravening one or more statutory provisions; or (b) has contravened a statutory provision and is likely to do so again.
- *Prohibition notices.* These require an activity which, in the inspector's opinion, involves a risk of serious personal injury to cease. There is no requirement for a specific breach of the HSWA 1974 or related regulations.

The Health and Safety (Offences) Act 2008 came into force on 16 January 2009 and increased the maximum penalties for health and safety offences under the HSWA 1974. The main change is that breaches of sections 2–6 of the HSWA 1974 not only carry financial penalties but now also may result in prison sentences.

13.9. Checklist of Do's and Don'ts

- Ensure that there is a policy on health and safety at work.
- Decide who in the organization is to be responsible for health and safety.
- Decide on the method of recording injuries and accidents at work.

14. IMMIGRATION, SECONDMENT AND FOREIGN ASSIGNMENT

14.1. Overview Laws Controlling Immigration

The immigration system in the UK is a points-based system whereby an individual's right to work in the UK is based on having a certain number of points, assigned by reference to factors such as qualifications, income and work experience. There are five tiers:

- Tier 1: high value migrants aimed at high value and highly skilled individuals who will contribute to the UK's productivity and growth.
- Tier 2: sponsored skilled workers with job offers who are coming to the UK to fill a gap in the UK labour market.
- Tier 3: low-skilled migrants who are recruited to fill specific temporary labour shortages (currently suspended as these jobs can be filled by nationals of the European Economic Area [EEA]).
- Tier 4: students.
- Tier 5: youth mobility and temporary or exchange migrants, coming to the UK for primarily non-economic reasons.

14.2. Recruiting, Screening and Hiring Process

It is advisable to make all offers of employment conditional upon presentation of documentation that proves that the applicant has the right to work in the UK. An employer may ask all applicants at the relevant stage of the recruitment process to produce evidence of entitlement to work in the UK and it will not commit an act of discrimination, provided that all applicants are subject to this requirement.

When checking immigrant status, an employer must take reasonable steps to verify the authenticity of the documents, for example by checking that any photograph or date of birth accords with the apparent appearance and age of the individual. The employer should also check the expiry dates of any leave to remain in the UK by examining any visa. A record should be kept of all documents examined.

British citizens are not subject to immigration control; however, citizens of British Dependant Territories and British Overseas citizens do require immigration permission to work in the UK. Nationals of the EEA and

Switzerland are free to live and work in the UK, but EEA nationals from eight of the countries which joined the EEA in May 2004 (Czech Republic, Estonia, Latvia, Lithuania, Hungary, Poland, Slovenia and Slovak Republic) are subject to the Workers Registration Scheme. Citizens of Romania and Bulgaria will not have an automatic right to work in the UK and for the time being must apply for a work permit and an accession worker card. All other individuals will need immigration permission to work in the UK under one of the five tiers of the points-based system, as listed above.

14.3. Obligation of Employer to Enforce Immigration Laws

Under the Immigration, Asylum and Nationality Act 2006 an employer commits a civil offence and is liable to pay a civil financial penalty if it employs a person aged 16 or over who is subject to immigration control and who has no permission to work in the UK, or who works for the employer in breach of their conditions of stay in the UK. If a person was recruited between 1 May 1997 and 28 February 2008, an employer has a statutory defence to the offence of employing an illegal migrant worker if it can show that it verified a person's right to work in the UK before employing them and was satisfied that the worker had permission to work in the UK.

If a person was recruited after 29 February 2008, employers are still liable to a civil penalty and there remains a very similar defence. However, the defence will only be available where the employer carries out repeated checks, at least once every twelve months. The documents that should be checked for staff employed from 29 February 2008 are described in the guidance booklets published by the UK Border Agency (UKBA).

An employer will commit a criminal offence if it knowingly employs someone who does not have permission to work in the UK; therefore, it is crucial for employers to abide by immigration laws and check that employees have the right to work in the UK. The criminal offence applies where an employer knowingly employs an adult subject to immigration control, who has not been granted leave to enter or remain in the UK, or whose leave is invalid, has ceased to have effect or is subjected to a condition preventing the person from accepting the employment.

Before an employer may employ a worker under Tiers 2, 4 and 5 the employer will have to first register with the UKBA in order to obtain a license, known as a sponsorship license. Under the license scheme, employers are given a status dependent on their immigration compliance. If an employer does not comply with immigration requirements they may be awarded a B-rated status, this means that they will be closely monitored by the UKBA. An employer who complies with the immigration rules will usually be awarded an A-rated status. The license must be renewed by the employer every four years.

Foreign nationals may visit the UK for up to six months as visitors. They may transact business during that time, but may not take up employment, whether paid or unpaid. The UKBA has provided guidance on what a business visitor is permitted to do, for example they may attend meetings, conduct negotiations and observe, but must not take employment or undertake anything which amounts to productive work. It is irrelevant that the individual is being paid overseas.

14.4. Fines and Penalties

The UK immigration rules provide that any application to enter or remain in the UK will be refused if deception is used, and that anyone seeking to come into the UK, in any capacity, who has previously breached immigration law may be barred from the UK for a fixed period (the length of time being dependent on the nature of the breach). Prospective employers should check with the individual if they have previously had any application to come to (or stay in) the UK refused or have ever been denied entry on arrival to the UK.

Under the old rules, applicable to employees employed from 1997 to 29 February 2008, there are both criminal and civil penalties. There remain today both criminal and civil penalties, but these were updated in the rules applicable from 29 February 2008.

If an illegal migrant worker is employed from 29 February 2008 and the employer does not have the defence of having verified the person's right to work in the UK, the employer could be liable for a civil penalty of up to GBP 10,000 per illegal worker. The amount of the penalty will be assessed on a sliding scale, taking into account a number of factors including the nature of the employer's checks, whether the employer reported suspected illegal migrants to the UKBA, the employer's cooperation with the UKBA and any previous offences by the employer.

The immigration officers have powers of arrest, entry and search. Employers, convicted of employing an illegal migrant worker will also be subject to criminal penalties, including up to two years' imprisonment and/or an unlimited fine. There is no statutory defence to the criminal penalty.

Under the Accession (Immigration and Worker Authorisation) Regulations 2006, an employer can be fined a maximum of GBP 5,000 per illegal worker for employing a non-exempt Bulgarian or Romanian who does not have permission to undertake the employment.

Failure by the employer to comply with the immigration rules could lead to their sponsorship license being down graded to a B-rated status or even the license being withdrawn, and could even mean that sponsored employees have to leave the UK.

14.5. Secondment/Foreign Assignment

Employees are able to come to the UK and remain here as intra-company transferees under Tier 2 of the Points-Based System, which would enable them to work in the UK. Under this tier, an employer can fill vacancies in its UK operations by bringing across some of its existing foreign-based staff. Workers coming to the UK in this way must be paid at the same rates as UK workers. With effect from April 2010 there are three types of intra-company transfer: established staff, skills transfer and graduate trainees.

14.6. Checklist of Do's and Don'ts

- Employers should carefully examine any documentation provided by prospective employees to ensure that they have the right to work in the UK.
- Employers should carry out checks every twelve months to verify the employee's right to work in the UK.

15. RESTRICTIVE COVENANTS AND PROTECTION OF TRADE SECRETS AND CONFIDENTIAL INFORMATION

15.1. Overview

Employees often gain knowledge of technology, strategic information about the employer's business or customer contacts that they may try to use for the benefit of their new employer or business. It is for this reason that restrictive covenants should be drafted into an employee's contract of employment.

15.2. The Law of Trade Secrets

Case law has developed and reinforced four kinds of business information. The category into which the relevant piece of information falls will govern the extent to which its owner can protect that information as well as the remedies available to it in the event of its disclosure. The following are the four categories of information:

- Trade secrets.
- Confidential information (sometimes known as 'mere confidential information').
- Information that amounts to the skill and knowledge of the employee.
- Public information.

The first category of information, trade secrets, can be protected both during and after the termination of employment, even if there is not an express covenant.

The next category, 'mere' confidential information, has been the subject of most of the case law in this area. Usually cases have involved employers seeking to elevate the information in question from the category of 'mere confidential information' to the more protectable category of a trade secret.

It is accepted widely that information in the last two categories (information that amounts to the general skill and knowledge of the employee and public information) is not proprietorial and is not therefore capable of protection.

Those attempting to protect confidential information should be as conversant as possible with the information itself, its purpose and its constituent parts. It is common for legal advisors simply to define 'confidential information' using pre-prepared lists of information that is likely to be confidential when drafting an employment contract or confidentiality agreement. Simply defining information as 'confidential' will not, however, be enough to make it so. The courts will examine the information, its provenance and purpose, and the damage it could do (or has done) to its owner if it were disclosed without authorization. They will then use this factual matrix to determine the proper status of the information, and the type and extent of protection to be afforded to it.

15.3. Restrictive Covenants and Non-compete Agreements

A contractual term restricting an employee's activities after termination is void for being in restraint of trade and contrary to public policy unless the employer can show that:

- it has a legitimate proprietary interest that it is appropriate to protect;
- the protection sought is no more than is reasonable having regard to the interests of the parties and the public interest.

An employer cannot impose a covenant merely to stop someone from competing, but it can seek to stop that person from using or damaging something which legitimately belongs to it.

There can be no guarantee that any restrictive covenant will be enforceable and there are no general guidelines which can be specified as to what would be considered reasonable, for example in terms of time or geography. Each clause must be considered in each case by reference to the business needs of the employer imposing the restriction.

Non-solicitation Covenants

Customers

There is generally no implied restriction on soliciting a former employer's customers. An employee's personal influence over customers may be dealt with by a covenant preventing an employee from soliciting the customers of the employer. The covenant should be restricted to customers with whom the employee had contact during a specified period before termination. In principle it is also possible to protect an interest in genuine prospective customers if they are sufficiently defined.

A non-solicitation restriction need not be limited to customers with whom the individual had direct contact. It can include those of whom the employee was aware, if it is intended to protect either the general customer base (where the identity of the employer's customers is not public knowledge but is known to the individual) or the general goodwill of the business (where that attaches specifically to the individual). If this is the aim, the restriction should be limited to:

- the period that the identity of customers will remain secret;
- the period that it will take for the individual's knowledge to go out of date; or
- the time until the goodwill ceases to attach to the individual and reverts to the employer.

Existing Employees

It is now reasonably well accepted that preventing a former employee from soliciting other employees may protect a legitimate interest in the stability of the workforce.

Non-dealing Covenants

A restriction on the solicitation of customers can be extended to cover not only enticement or interference (where active steps are required by the individual) but also the provision of services (where no active steps are required: the customer could approach the individual). This is known as a non-dealing covenant and has clear advantages as regards enforceability, because it avoids the need to prove that the individual made an approach, which is usually hard to prove in practice. However, it does significantly broaden the prohibition, not only to affect the rights of the employee in question but also those of third parties, so a court is more likely to be cautious about enforcing it.

The enforceability of a non-dealing covenant will depend on the interest being protected. Similar considerations as for the enforcement of non-solicitation covenants will generally apply.

The non-dealing covenant will not be enforceable if it prevents any contact with the relevant business contacts. The restriction must be focused on contact with those business contacts that would affect the employer's business.

The employment

Employees are restricted as a matter of general law from disclosing confidential information amounting to a trade secret (e.g., a manufacturing process) after termination and can be made subject to express confidentiality provisions.

A non-competition restriction has traditionally been harder to enforce than a non-solicitation restriction, since it represents a greater infringement of the general principle that covenants in restraint of trade are illegal.

However, a non-competition restriction is likely to be enforced in certain circumstances:

- It may not be possible to give the legitimate proprietary interest, for example a manufacturing process or confidential trade secret, sufficient protection through the implied and express confidentiality terms. A restriction against carrying out the activity is then more realistic, and easier to police.
- The individual's influence over customers or suppliers may be so great that the only effective protection is to ensure that they are not engaged in a competing business in any way.

The courts have confirmed that they are prepared to enforce non-competition covenants. As with non-solicitation covenants, the restriction must be for a limited time. When deciding the appropriate period it is necessary to consider how long it will be before competitive activities by the individual represent less than a material threat to the legitimate interest. For example, how long will it be before the manufacturing process changes so much that the individual's knowledge of it is out of date?

The geographical extent of the limitation must also be considered. A longer lasting restriction or one that covers a wider geographical area necessarily represents a greater restriction on trading. Relevant factors to determine whether the geographical scope is reasonable will include:

- whether there is an actual relationship between the interest to be protected and any specific geographical area;
- the area of activities of the employee;
- the size and nature of the population of the area.

Examples of Restrictive Covenants

In order to protect the Confidential Information to which he has access as a result of the Employment, the Employee covenants with the Company [(for itself and as trustee and agent for each Group Company)] that he shall not:

- for [PERIOD] months after Termination, solicit or endeavour to entice away from the Company [or any Group Company] the business or custom

of a Restricted Customer with a view to providing goods or services to that Restricted Customer in competition with any Restricted Business; or
- for [PERIOD] months after Termination [in the course of any business concern which is in competition with any Restricted Business], offer to employ or engage or otherwise endeavour to entice away from the Company [or any Group Company] any Restricted Person; or
- for [PERIOD] months after Termination, be involved in any Capacity with any business concern which is (or intends to be) in competition with any Restricted Business; or
- for [PERIOD] months after Termination, be involved with the provision of goods or services to (or otherwise have any business dealings with) any Restricted Customer in the course of any business concern which is in competition with any Restricted Business; or
- at any time after Termination, represent himself as connected with the Company [or any Group Company] in any Capacity.

None of the restrictions in clause [] shall prevent the Employee from:

- holding an investment by way of shares or other securities of not more than [5]% of the total issued share capital of any company, whether or not it is listed or dealt in on a recognized stock exchange; or
- being engaged or concerned in any business concern insofar as the Employee's duties or work shall relate solely to geographical areas where the business concern is not in competition with any Restricted Business; or
- [being engaged or concerned in any business concern, provided that the Employee's duties or work shall relate solely to services or activities of a kind with which the Employee was not concerned to a material extent in the [PERIOD] months prior to Termination.]

The restrictions imposed on the Employee by this clause 2 apply to him acting:

- directly or indirectly; and
- on his own behalf or on behalf of, or in conjunction with, any firm, company or person.

The period[s] for which the restriction[s] in clause [] apply shall be reduced by any period that the Employee spends on Garden Leave (i.e., where an employee serves a period of notice at home. She/he remains employed but is prevented from working, contacting clients, contacts or other employees) immediately prior to Termination.

The Company and the Employee entered into the restrictions in this clause 2 having been separately legally advised.

Each of the restrictions in this clause [] is intended to be separate and severable. If any of the restrictions shall be held to be void but would be valid if part of their wording were deleted, such restriction shall apply with such deletion as may be necessary to make it valid or effective.

The Employee will, at the request and expense of the Company, enter into a separate agreement with any Group Company in which he agrees to be bound by restrictions corresponding to those restrictions in this clause [] (or such of those restrictions as may be appropriate) in relation to that Group Company.

15.4. Checklist of Do's and Don'ts

- Consider which posts bring employees into contact with customers and clients and/or expose them to confidential information (particularly the type that could damage the business if disclosed), and draft appropriate covenants into those employees' contracts.
- Avoid adopting a blanket system of including restrictive covenants in all employee contracts, even for employees whose jobs do not bring them into contact with clients or expose them to confidential information.
- Ensure that the drafting of the covenants is aimed at protecting legitimate business interests and not simply at preventing competition.

16. PROTECTION OF WHISTLEBLOWING CLAIMS

16.1. Overview

The Public Interest Disclosure Act 1998 (PIDA) provides protection from victimization or dismissal for workers who report malpractices by their employers or third parties. The introduction of PIDA led to many employers introducing whistleblowing policies to encourage internal disclosure and to resolve malpractices to which PIDA applies.

PIDA creates two levels of protection for whistleblowers. The dismissal of an employee will be automatically unfair if the reason, or principal reason, for their dismissal is that they have made a 'protected disclosure'. PIDA also protects workers from being subjected to any detriment on the ground that they have made a 'protected disclosure'.

There is no financial cap on compensation in whistleblowing claims, and no requirement for a minimum period of service.

A whistleblower qualifies for protection if there is a qualifying disclosure, and there is a protected disclosure.

Have They Made a Qualifying Disclosure?

The PIDA sets out a number of requirements for a qualifying disclosure:

- The worker must make a disclosure of information. Merely gathering evidence or threatening to make a disclosure is not sufficient.
- The information must relate to one of six types of 'relevant failure':
  - (a) Criminal offences.
  - (b) Breach of any legal obligation.
  - (c) Miscarriages of justice.
  - (d) Danger to the health and safety of any individual.
  - (e) Damage to the environment.
  - (f) The employer must have deliberate concealed information about any of the above.
- The worker must have a reasonable belief that the information tends to show one of the relevant failures.

Is It Also a Protected Disclosure?

The disclosure must also qualify as a protected disclosure which broadly depends on:

- The identity of the person to whom disclosure is made. PIDA encourages disclosure to the worker's employer (internal disclosure) as the primary method of whistleblowing. Disclosure to third parties (external disclosure) may be protected if more stringent conditions are met.
- Other conditions. Disclosure to the employer is protected provided it is made in good faith. Further conditions for disclosure to third parties depend on the identity of the third party. Disclosure to a 'responsible' third party, or a 'prescribed person' is likely to gain protection relatively easily. However, wider disclosures, such as to the police or to the media, will only qualify in very limited cases.

16.2. Checklist of Do's and Don'ts

- Ensure that there is a clear procedure should employees wish to 'blow the whistle' and complain about working practices or other matters set out in the PIDA.
- Put the whistleblowing procedure in writing and make it readily available to all employees.
- Promote a working culture whereby employees feel that they can raise concerns without fear of adverse reaction or consequences.
- Train managers on how to deal with a whistleblowing claim.
- Do not punish an employee or subject him or her to any detriment as a result of blowing the whistle.

17. PROHIBITION OF DISCRIMINATION IN THE WORKPLACE

17.1. Overview of Discrimination Laws in England

Summary

Discrimination law in England prohibits discrimination on a number of different grounds, in all facets of employment including recruitment, contractual terms, working conditions, promotions, transfers, dismissals and training. The law protects employees (in a broad sense), former employees and applicants for employment, as well as a range of non-employed individuals, such as agency workers, office-holders and partners. While the law primarily governs the conduct of employers, others may also be held personally liable where they have played a part in the discrimination.

Different discrimination laws (see below) have been introduced in England since 1975 when the Sex Discrimination Act 1975 came into force and continuing until 2006 when age discrimination laws were introduced for the first time. In April 2010 the many different strands of discrimination law were brought together into one Act with the introduction of the Equality Act 2010 ('EA 2010').

Discrimination law protects a wide range of individuals within the field of employment, occupation and vocational training. The term 'employment' is defined for the purposes of discrimination law as working under a contract of service or apprenticeship, or a contract personally to perform any work. It includes employees and workers. However, it also covers those who are genuinely self-employed, provided the contract obliges them to perform the work personally (in other words, if they are not permitted to subcontract any part of the work or employ their own staff to do it).

Discrimination in Employment

In terms of employment related discrimination, an employer must not discriminate against an employee in any of the following ways:

- In the terms of employment offered. This makes it unlawful for an employer to discriminate in the contractual terms of employment, whether they be express or implied.
- In affording an employee access to opportunities for promotion, transfer or training, or by deliberately denying him such opportunities. Employers should be aware that internal promotion poses a risk of unlawful discrimination as often it involves subjective managerial assessment.
- In affording an employee access to any other benefits, facilities or services or by deliberately denying him access to such benefits. This includes pay,

mobility, holiday, pension, and other fringe benefits such as opportunities to work overtime. It can also relate to a failure to deal with an employee's grievance adequately or dealing with an employee's grievance but with an unreasonable amount of delay.
- By dismissing an employee. This includes termination of a contract by the employer (with or without notice) and non-renewal or expiry of a fixed term contract. Criteria used for dismissal, including in selection for redundancies, must not be directly or indirectly discriminatory.
- By subjecting the employee to any other detriment. 'Subject to detriment' means that the employee might take the view that he has been disadvantaged in the circumstances in which he has to work, although the disadvantage must amount to something more than an unjustified sense of grievance.

Grounds for Discrimination

For discussions of situations in which discrimination may be permissible, see the sections on specific types of discrimination below.

17.1.1. Direct Discrimination

A person (A) directly discriminates against another person (B) if because of a protected characteristic, A treats B less favourably that A treats, or would treat, others.

Protected characteristics are:

- Age
- Disability
- Gender re-assignment
- Marriage and civil partnership
- Pregnancy and maternity
- Race
- Religion or belief
- Sex
- Sexual orientation.

Direct discrimination is based on the concept of less favourable treatment. Merely treating two people differently does not, of itself, mean that one has been treated less favourably than the other. However, B does not need to show that the treatment is 'objectively' worse; it is sufficient if B 'could reasonably say that he would have preferred not to have been treated differently'.

To be guilty of direct discrimination, A must treat B less favourably than A treats, or would treat, a comparator. The comparator must be someone whose 'relevant circumstances are the same or not materially different' from those of B. The 'relevant circumstances' are those factors (not including the allegedly discriminatory factor) which A has taken into account in deciding to treat B in that way. Where no appropriate real comparator can be identified (or the claimant fails on their case based on a real comparator), the tribunal has a duty to consider whether a case could be made out based on a 'hypothetical comparator'.

The only exception to the rule requiring a comparator for direct discrimination is with pregnancy and maternity discrimination. Direct discrimination because of pregnancy and maternity simply requires that the employee is treated unfavourably because of the pregnancy or due to the fact that she has taken maternity leave.

Generally direct discrimination cannot be justified. The only types of direct discrimination that can be justified are disability and age discrimination.

It is interesting to note that with the new definitions of direct discrimination introduced by the EA 2010, the protected characteristic does not need to relate to the person complaining of discrimination. This, in effect, formalizes an area of law that was introduced when more recent strands of discrimination were introduced (sexual orientation) and has developed through disability discrimination case law – the concept of discrimination by association and perception.

17.1.2. Indirect Discrimination

The concept of indirect discrimination recognizes that some practices that appear to treat people equally may nevertheless adversely affect some groups (defined by reference to sex, marital status, race, religion or belief, sexual orientation or age) more than others. Indirect discrimination will be unlawful unless it can be objectively justified. For example, a requirement that you must be 6 feet 3 inches tall would place women at a disadvantage when compared to men and therefore would indirectly discriminate against women. Such a policy will be unlawful unless it the height requirement can be justified.

A common example of indirect discrimination is an employer requiring all employees to work full-time. This requirement has a disproportionate impact on women, since women in society as a whole bear a greater part of domestic and childcare responsibilities than men, and are more likely to want (or need) to work part-time. Therefore, if a woman wishes to work part-time, and the employer cannot objectively justify the need for a full-time worker to do the job, a requirement to work full-time would indirectly discriminate against her.

Generally speaking, a person (A) indirectly discriminates against another (B) where:

- A applies to B a provision, criterion or practice (PCP);
- A applies or would apply the PCP equally to persons with whom B does not share the relevant protected characteristic;
- the PCP puts or would put persons with whom B shares the protected characteristic at a particular disadvantage when compared with persons with whom B does not share the characteristic;
- the PCP puts, or would put, B at that disadvantage;
- the PCP is not a proportionate means of achieving a legitimate aim.

Until the introduction of the EA 2010 there had been no provision for claiming indirect disability discrimination. The EA 2010 introduced this for the first time.

A PCP will not be indirectly discriminatory where the employer can show that the PCP in question is a 'proportionate means of achieving a legitimate aim'. There is also no direct discrimination on grounds of age where the age-based criterion is a proportionate means of achieving a legitimate aim. This is known as objective justification.

For indirect discrimination (or direct discrimination based on age), the burden is on the employer to prove justification, and it is for the tribunal to apply its own discretion as to whether the treatment was justified.

17.1.3. Victimization

The prohibition on victimization is intended to ensure that victims and witnesses are not deterred from speaking out against discrimination or harassment for fear of reprisals. Victimization is usually committed by an employer who has been the subject of a discrimination complaint by a current or former employee, but this need not always be the case. For example, a prospective new employer can be liable for victimization if it refuses to employ someone who has given evidence against a previous employer in a discrimination case. Victimization is itself a form of discrimination, and so any reference to discrimination in the legislation will include victimization, unless otherwise indicated. Protection from victimization exists in all strands of discrimination law.

Victimization occurs where a person (A) subjects B to a detriment because (a) B does a protected act, or (b) A believes that B has done, or may do, a protected act. Under the new definition provided by the EA 2010 there is no need for a comparator.

The following are protected acts:

- bringing discrimination or equal pay proceedings against any person;
- giving evidence or information in connection with discrimination or equal pay proceedings brought by or against anybody;

- alleging that any person has committed an act which (whether or not the allegation so states) would amount to a contravention of the discrimination or equal pay legislation;
- otherwise doing anything under or by reference to the discrimination or equal pay legislation in relation to any person.

Making an allegation or giving information that later turns out to be false can still constitute a protected act, provided it was done in good faith. In contrast, a discrimination claim with no merit brought solely to harass the employer is not a protected act, as it is not brought in good faith.

17.1.4. Harassment

A person (A) harasses another person (B) where A engages in unwanted conduct:

- related to a relevant characteristic; and
- which has the purpose or effect of violating B's dignity; or
- creating an intimidating, hostile, degrading, humiliating or offensive environment for B.

A also harasses B if:

- A engages in unwanted conduct related to a relevant protected characteristic; and
- the conduct has the purpose or effect of violating B's dignity; or
- creating an intimidating, hostile, degrading, humiliating or offensive environment for B.

A also harasses B if:

- A engages in unwanted conduct of a sexual nature, and
- the conduct has the purpose or effect referred to above.

A also harasses B if:

- A or another person engages in unwanted conduct of a sexual nature or that is related to gender re-assignment or sex;
- the conduct has the purpose or effect referred to above; and
- because of B's rejection of or submission to the conduct, A treats B less favourably than A would treat B if B had not rejected or submitted to the conduct.

In deciding whether conduct has the effect referred to above, each of the following must be taken into account:

- the perception of B;
- the other circumstances of the case;
- whether it is reasonable for the conduct to have that effect.

Instructions to Discriminate

It is also unlawful for a person with authority over another (such as an employer) to give an instruction to commit unlawful discrimination, or to procure or attempt to procure the commission of such discrimination. Where instructions to discriminate amount to unwanted conduct that has the purpose or effect of violating the dignity of the employee, or of creating an intimidating, hostile, degrading, humiliating or offensive environment for them, this may give rise to liability for harassment. However, there is still the need to establish the necessary 'ground' or 'reason' for the conduct, that is, on the grounds of sex, race, age, disability, etc.

Bringing a Discrimination Claim

Time Limits

A discrimination claim must usually be submitted to an employment tribunal before the end of 'the period of three months beginning when the act complained of was done' (the normal time limit). Acts occurring more than three months before the claim is brought may still form the basis of the claim if they are part of a 'continuing act'. Regardless of whether there is a continuing act, time can be extended by the tribunal where it is just and equitable to do so.

Burden of Proof in Discrimination Cases

The task of proving a discrimination case lies initially on the claimant. They must prove facts from which the tribunal could conclude, in the absence of an adequate explanation, that the respondent has committed an act of unlawful discrimination or harassment (the 'prima facie' case).

However, once the claimant establishes a prima facie case, the tribunal must uphold the complaint unless the respondent proves that he did not commit or is not to be treated as having committed that act. The burden of proof applies in both direct and indirect discrimination cases.

17.1.5. Remedies and Compensation

In a successful discrimination claim, a tribunal must make one or more of the following orders where it considers it 'just and equitable' to do so:

- A declaration of the rights of the parties.
- An order that the respondent pay compensation to the claimant.
- A recommendation as to what steps the respondent should take to reduce the adverse effect of the discrimination on the claimant.

In practice, compensation is always (or very nearly always) awarded in successful discrimination cases. In determining the amount of compensation, the following general principles apply:

- Compensation can be awarded for financial losses (including loss of earnings, pension, and benefits in kind and any out-of-pocket expenses) and non-financial losses (including injury to feelings, personal injury and aggravated damages).
- Compensation is based on the tortious measure of damage and so should be calculated so as to put the claimant in the position they would have been in if the unlawful discrimination had not taken place.
- However, unlike damages in tort, the principles of remoteness do not apply, and so there is no requirement for the loss suffered to be reasonably foreseeable.
- Claimants are required to take reasonable steps to mitigate their losses.
- There is no upper limit on the amount of compensation that can be awarded.
- Compensation can be awarded against the employer and against any individual respondents, such as other employees.

17.2. Age Discrimination

Age discrimination applies to vocational training and all facets of employment, including recruitment, terms and conditions, promotions, transfers, dismissals and training. It covers employees, applicants for employment and former employees. Under age discrimination legislation, it is unlawful for an employer to:

- discriminate directly by treating another person less favourably than others because of age, where this cannot be objectively justified (direct discrimination);
- discriminate indirectly by applying a provision, criterion or practice that disadvantages people of a particular age, where this cannot be objectively justified (indirect discrimination);
- subject someone to harassment on grounds of age;
- victimize someone because they have made or intend to make a complaint or allegation or have given evidence against someone else in relation to a complaint of age discrimination.

Discrimination may be permitted in certain limited circumstances:

- An employer might be able to rely on a genuine occupational requirement (GOR) for an employee to possess a characteristic related to age.
- 'Positive action' might be allowed in the form of targeted advertising or training to address existing inequalities.

- An employer can dismiss an employee by reason of retirement at or over the default retirement age of 65.
- An employer might be able to award benefits based on length of service.

Age discrimination legislation provides that the dismissal of an employee aged 65 or over shall not be unlawful age discrimination 'where the reason for the dismissal is retirement'. The law sets out a procedure whereby employers must notify employees of their intended retirement date and consider a request by the employee not to be retired. Breach of this procedure does not of itself render a retirement dismissal discriminatory. Broadly speaking, the key issues are whether the employee has reached the normal retirement age (if any) for the job in question, and whether the employer has given the necessary written notice of the intended retirement date. If notice was not given, the dismissal is deemed not to be by reason of retirement.

17.3. Race Discrimination

It is unlawful to discriminate against someone on racial grounds such as colour, race, nationality or ethnic or national origins.

The law applies to vocational training and all facets of employment, including recruitment, terms and conditions, promotions, transfers, dismissals and training. It covers employees, applicants for employment and former employees. It is unlawful to:

- discriminate directly by treating another person less favourably than others because of race (direct discrimination);
- discriminate indirectly by applying a provision, criterion or practice that disadvantages people of a particular racial group, without justification (indirect discrimination);
- victimize someone because they have made or intend to make a complaint or allegation or have given evidence against someone else in relation to a complaint of race discrimination (victimization);
- subject someone to racial harassment (harassment).

Discrimination may be permitted in certain limited circumstances. For example:

- if there is a GOR for the worker to be of, for example, a particular ethnic origin in order to do the job; or
- 'positive action' may be permitted in the form of targeted advertising or training to address existing inequalities.

Where discrimination or harassment has been committed by an employee, the employer will usually be liable unless it has taken reasonable steps to prevent such conduct from taking place. The offending employee may also be liable.

Direct discrimination is prohibited if it is carried out on 'racial grounds'. Indirect discrimination can occur under where an employer's actions affect persons in the same 'racial group'. The term 'racial grounds' is defined as meaning on the grounds of colour, race, nationality or ethnic or national origins. Similarly, the law provides that a 'racial group' is a group of people defined by reference to colour, race, nationality or ethnic or national origins.

Colour has not been defined by the tribunals or courts, largely because the term is self-explanatory. Discrimination on the basis of colour may also include other grounds for the discrimination, for example, ethnic or national origins.

There are a few cases where the concept of 'race' is not easy to define. Given that the term 'ethnic origin' has been interpreted in a wider sense than 'strictly racial or biological', the precise definition of the term 'race' in this context is not of great importance.

It is clear from case law that 'ethnic origin' is wider than 'racial origin'. Discrimination against a member of an ethnic group can be taken as encompassing religious and cultural differences as well as strictly racial differences.

17.4. Sex Discrimination/Sexual Harassment

Sex discrimination legislation applies to all facets of employment, including recruitment, terms and conditions, promotions, transfers, dismissals and training. It covers employees, applicants for employment and former employees. It also prohibits discrimination in goods, facilities and services, which are outside the scope of this note.

It is unlawful to:

- discriminate directly by treating another person less favourably because of sex (direct discrimination);
- discriminate indirectly by applying a provision, criterion or practice that disadvantages people of a particular sex, without justification (indirect discrimination);
- victimize someone because they have made or intend to make a complaint or allegation or have given evidence against someone else in relation to a complaint of sex discrimination (victimization);
- subject someone to harassment related to sex or harassment of a sexual nature (harassment).

Discrimination may be permitted in certain limited circumstances, such as where being of a particular sex is a genuine occupational qualification.

Where discrimination or harassment has been committed by an employee, the employer will usually be liable unless it has taken reasonable steps to prevent such conduct from taking place. The offending employee may also be liable.

17.5. Handicap and Disability Discrimination

Discrimination legislation prohibits discrimination against those with disabilities and creates certain obligations on employers when faced with an employee with a disability.

While there are some similarities in approach to other strands of discrimination law, there are two significant differences:

- Only persons with a condition falling within the definition of 'disability' set out in EA 2010 qualify for its protection.
- Uniquely in domestic discrimination law, it imposes obligations on employers to treat disabled persons more favourably in certain circumstances.

The following types of discriminatory behaviour are prohibited:

- Direct discrimination.
- Disability-related discrimination.
- Discrimination arising from disability.
- Failure to comply with a duty to make reasonable adjustments.
- Victimization.
- Harassment.
- Instructions or pressure to discriminate.
- Aiding an unlawful act.

Discrimination Arising from Disability

The EA 2010 introduced a new type of disability discrimination: *discrimination arising from disability*. This means that where a person (A) treats a person (B) unfavourably because of something arising in consequence of B's disability and A cannot justify the treatment. An employer faced with a claim of discrimination arising from disability has a defence if he did not know, and could not reasonably have been expected to know, that B had the disability.

Failure to Comply with a Duty to Make a Reasonable Adjustment

The law imposes a duty on employers to make reasonable adjustments to premises or working practices to take account of the needs of a disabled employee or job applicant.

Where 'a provision, criterion or practice applied by or on behalf of an employer, or any physical feature of premises occupied by the employer, places the disabled person concerned at a substantial disadvantage in comparison with persons who are not disabled, it is the duty of the employer to take such steps as it is reasonable, in all the circumstances of the case, for him to have to take in order to prevent the provision, criterion or practice, or physical feature, having that effect'.

A failure to make reasonable adjustments is classed as a form of discrimination in itself. Furthermore, an employer will not be able to justify disability-related discrimination (see *above*) where there were reasonable adjustments which could have been made, unless the employer shows that, even with those adjustments, the discrimination would still have been justified.

Indirect Discrimination

Prior to the introduction of the EA 2010, indirect discrimination had not applied to disability discrimination. However with the introduction on the new Act, indirect disability discrimination now applies to disability discrimination in the same way that it does other strands of discrimination law.

Meaning of Disability

A person has a disability if he has a physical or mental impairment which has a substantial and long-term effect on his ability to carry out normal day-to-day activities.

17.6. National Origin Discrimination

The law prohibits discrimination on the grounds of nationality, which is defined to include citizenship. It is not limited to the legal nationality acquired at birth but can include a change in nationality due to marriage.

17.7. Religious Discrimination

One major point of debate since the introduction of laws prohibiting discrimination on the grounds of religion and belief is the definition of what constitutes a 'religion or belief'. 'Religion or belief' means as follows:

- 'Religion' means any religion.
- 'Belief' means any religious or philosophical belief.
- A reference to religion includes a reference to lack of religion.
- A reference to belief includes a reference to lack of belief.

Issues of indirect discrimination have also presented challenges, since they have involved courts in balancing the needs of business and the needs of different religious groups. For example, an employer's refusal to pay an employee extra for work on a week day which their religion treats as the Sabbath could arguably amount to indirect discrimination if the employer pays double time to those who work on Sundays or on other Christian holidays (such as Easter or Christmas).

There is also scope for potential conflict between the laws prohibiting discrimination on the grounds of Religion or Belief and Sexual Orientation since some religious groups have strong views on homosexuality.

The religion and belief discrimination laws apply to vocational training and all facets of employment, including recruitment, terms and conditions, promotions, transfers, dismissals and training. They cover employees, applicants for employment and former employees. It is unlawful on the grounds of religion or belief to:

- discriminate directly by treating another person less favourably than others because of their religion or belief (direct discrimination);
- discriminate indirectly by applying a provision, criterion or practice that disadvantages people of a particular religion or belief without good reason (indirect discrimination);
- victimize someone because they have made or intend to make a complaint or allegation or have given evidence against someone else in relation to a complaint of discrimination on the grounds of religion or belief (victimization);
- subject someone to harassment (harassment).

Discrimination may be permitted in certain limited circumstances:

- If there is a GOR for the worker to be of a particular religion or belief in order to do the job.
- To comply with the religious or belief-based ethos of the organization.
- Special rules apply if the job is for a teacher in a denominational school.
- Special rules apply to Sikhs working on building sites.
- 'Positive action' may be permitted in the form of targeted advertising or training to address existing inequalities.
- Cases involving national security.

Where discrimination or harassment has been committed by an employee, the employer will usually be liable unless it has taken reasonable steps to prevent such conduct from taking place. The offending employee may also be liable.

17.8. Military Status Discrimination

Discrimination laws in England do no not currently prohibit discrimination on the grounds of military status.

17.9. Pregnancy and Maternity Discrimination

It is unlawful to discriminate against a woman if, in the protected period in relation to a pregnancy of hers, her employer treats her unfavourably:

- because of the pregnancy;
- because of illness suffered by her as a result of it;
- because she is on compulsory maternity leave;
- because she is exercising or seeking to exercise, or has exercised or sought to exercise, the right to ordinary or AML.

Dismissal for a reason related to pregnancy is also automatically unfair.

17.10. Marital Status Discrimination

The law prohibits direct and indirect discrimination against married people of either sex on the grounds of their marital or civil partner status. There is no parallel protection for unmarried people.

The Civil Partnership Act 2004, which came into effect on 5 December 2005, amended the law so that civil partners have the same status as spouses and may not be discriminated against on grounds of their civil partner status. For example, any benefits such as private medical insurance, provided by employers to employees' spouses must also be extended to employee's civil partners.

17.11. Sexual Orientation Discrimination

The laws prohibiting discrimination on the grounds of sexual orientation apply to vocational training and all facets of employment, including recruitment, terms and conditions, promotions, transfers, dismissals and training. They make it unlawful to:

- discriminate directly by treating another person less favourably than others because of their actual or perceived sexual orientation (direct discrimination);
- discriminate indirectly by applying a provision, criterion or practice that disadvantages people of a particular sexual orientation without objective justification (indirect discrimination);
- victimize someone for making a complaint or giving evidence against someone else in relation to a complaint under the Sexual Orientation Regulations (victimization);
- harass a person on the ground of sexual orientation (harassment);
- discriminate against or harass someone after the working relationship has ended.

Exceptions may be made in very limited circumstances:

- If there is a GOR for the worker to be of a particular sexual orientation in order to do the job.
- Where the employment is for purposes of an organized religion an employer may apply a requirement relating to sexual orientation for limited specified reasons.
- On the grounds of national security or positive action.
- Where benefits are prevented or restricted by reference to marital or civil partner status.
- Where discrimination or harassment is proved, an employer may not be held liable if it has taken reasonable steps to prevent such conduct from taking place.

'Sexual Orientation' is defined as 'a sexual orientation towards persons of the same sex; persons of the opposite sex; or persons of the same sex and of the opposite sex'. The law therefore provides protection for gay men, lesbians, bisexuals and heterosexuals.

A sexual orientation is simply an orientation towards persons of the same or opposite sex, or both sexes. The definition does not include particular sexual practices, nor preferences for particular types of sexual activity, such as sadomasochism or bestiality. Neither would it appear to cover celibacy.

17.12. Retaliation

Retaliation is a term that is equivalent to victimisation under English discrimination laws. This is dealt with above.

17.13. Constructive Discharge

Referred to as a constructive dismissal under English law, this occurs where the employer does not dismiss the employee, but the employee resigns and can show that they were entitled to do so by virtue of the employer's conduct. Acts of discrimination invariably entitle an employee to resign and claim to have been constructively dismissed.

17.14. Checklist of Do's and Don'ts

- Adopt an Equal Opportunities Policy dealing with all aspects of discrimination in the workplace.
- Ensure that managers are trained on equal opportunity issues in the workplace.

18. SMOKING IN THE WORKPLACE

18.1. Overview

On 19 July 2006, the Health Act 2006 (HA 2006) introduced a ban on smoking at work in England.

It is now a criminal offence to smoke in a smoke-free place. Employers and others who manage smoke-free premises must put up no-smoking signs and prevent smoking or face criminal sanctions.

The smoking ban covers the following premises:

- Premises open to the public, whether by invitation or not, and whether upon payment or not. The smoking ban apples only while the premises are open to the public, unless they are also a workplace.
- Premises used as a place of work (including voluntary work) by more than one person, even if those who work there do so at different times, or only intermittently. The smoking ban applies at all times.
- Premises used as a place of work (including voluntary work) where members of the public, or a section of the public, might attend for the purpose of seeking or receiving goods or services from those working there, even if members of the public are not always present. These premises must be smoke-free at all times.

In the employment context it will be a defence if an employee can show that they s/he did not know, and could not reasonably have been expected to know, that the workplace was a smoke-free place. The employee only has to adduce sufficient evidence to raise the issue, and the court will assume that the defence is satisfied. The onus is then on the prosecution to prove beyond a reasonable doubt that the defence is not satisfied. Anyone found guilty of smoking in a smoke-free premises will be liable to pay a fine of up to GBP 200.

Anyone who controls or is concerned in the management of smoke-free premises (in the employment context, the employer) has a duty to stop anyone from smoking on the premises. A failure to comply with this duty is also an offence. Anyone charged with the offence will have a defence if they can show one of the following:

- They took reasonable steps to cause the person in question to stop smoking.
- They did not know, and could not reasonably have been expected to know, that the person in question was smoking.
- It was reasonable on other grounds for them not to comply with the duty.

A person found guilty of this offence will be liable to pay a fine of up to GBP 2,500 on conviction in a Magistrates' court.

Employers must ensure that no-smoking signs are correctly displayed. A failure to comply with this duty is an offence punishable by fine of up to GBP 1,000.

18.2. Checklist of Do's and Don'ts

- Draft a 'no-smoking' policy and ensure that all employees are aware of it.
- Ensure that 'no-smoking' signs are correctly displayed.
- Create a disciplinary offence, punishable by summary dismissal, for smoking in the workplace.

19. USE OF DRUGS AND ALCOHOL IN THE WORKPLACE

19.1. Overview of Laws and Regulations in England

Employees whose performance, behaviour or attendance at work is affected by alcohol or drugs are subject to dismissal, generally at the employer's discretion, on the ground of misconduct. However, drinking or drug taking, either on or off duty, may also be a fair reason for dismissal on grounds of capability.

There is an increasing trend towards treating long-term alcoholism and, to a lesser extent, dependence on illegal drugs, as serious illnesses. There is a line of thinking that suggests that drug and alcohol misuse should be seen as a health problem, and that employees should be supported as far as possible, with disciplinary action being used only as a last resort. Similarly, ACAS suggests that employers should consider introducing measures to help employees who are suffering from the effects of alcohol or drug abuse. The aim should be to identify affected employees and encourage them to seek help and treatment.

If a problem with alcohol or drugs is a symptom of a disability, the employee may be protected under the Disability Discrimination Act 1995. However, if drinking and drug misconduct cause the employee to recklessly or even deliberately disregard company rules or acceptable standards of conduct, employers may be justified in adopting a less tolerant approach.

Alcoholism

Where an employee's drinking is associated with a medical condition, misdemeanours such as lateness, erratic behaviour or poor performance will often result from that medical problem. In such instances, the employer will probably refrain from disciplining the employee for the misconduct and deal instead with the root cause. However, manifestations of the illness in the form of gross misconduct may still be treated as such, and tribunals recognize that employers can reach the point where they are entitled to say 'enough is enough'. Alcoholism itself is not a disability within the meaning of the DDA, but its potential causes and effects may be.

Drug Dependency

Drug addiction, like alcoholism, should in theory be treated as an illness, but tribunals have almost invariably regarded drug-related dismissals as a misconduct issue. This may be because the use of controlled drugs is a criminal offence. Furthermore, employers themselves can commit an offence under the Misuse of Drugs Act 1971 if they know that illegal drugs are being used or distributed on their premises.

The fact that an employee has committed a criminal offence does not necessarily mean that an employer can dismiss for misconduct. If an employer finds out about a conviction for a previous drug offence and dismisses the employee as a result, the dismissal for failing to disclose the conviction may be unfair if it has become 'spent' under section 4(3)(b) of the Rehabilitation of Offenders Act 1974. Employees do not have to declare spent convictions on a job application.

Drinking and Drug Taking while on Duty

As stated above, in certain circumstances it may be appropriate for employers to treat alcohol or drug abuse as an illness. At the other extreme, there are more straightforward cases of drink and drug misconduct where the employee recklessly or even deliberately disregards company rules or acceptable standards of conduct. Here employers may be justified in adopting a less tolerant approach, especially where there is a company rule identifying drunkenness and drug use at work as meriting dismissal.

Giving an employee the chance to respond fully and thoughtfully to allegations will mean taking him or her off work and not holding an interview until he or she sobers up. Note that even where employers seek to rely on conduct as the reason for dismissal, the requirement of carrying out a reasonable investigation may mean that they should seek medical advice about the employee's condition.

It is for a tribunal to assess whether an employee's dismissal for misconduct was a reasonable response under ERA 1996. Matters taken into account include the size and administrative resources of the employer, the employee's seniority, and any responsibilities held by the employee, in particular in relation to health and safety.

Tribunals take a very strict view of alcohol and drug-related misconduct where considerations of health and safety are involved. Employers have obligations under common law and various statutes, notably the Health and Safety at Work Act 1974, to keep their employees safe. Employers are obliged to take reasonable steps to ensure that their employees are not acting under the influence of alcohol or drugs if this is likely to give rise to a risk to the health and safety of others, and employees themselves have a duty not to injure their colleagues.

When the nature of the employee's work is such that the consumption of alcohol or drugs gives rise to serious safety risks, dismissal may be fair, even where there is no specific rule dealing with alcohol or drugs.

There may be an absolute prohibition on the possession of drugs and alcohol where safety considerations are paramount, for example, on ships and oil rigs. Workplaces that afford easy access to alcohol and drugs may also have specific rules prohibiting possession on the premises. The primary intention here is often to discourage theft of the employer's property. However, such rules should not be applied in an over-rigid manner.

Drug and Alcohol Testing

The extent to which employers have the right to require employees to undertake random drug or alcohol testing is limited. Some employers reserve the contractual right to test their staff randomly in contracts of employment. If an employee has accepted this and then refuses a test, he or she will be in breach of contract. In the absence of a contractual term, employers cannot require employees to take an alcohol or drug test unless there are legitimate safety concerns.

Employers should be wary of unnecessarily invading the privacy of their employees as it can leave them open to legal challenges, particularly under Human Rights legislation and the DPA. The testing procedure itself is highly invasive. The obtaining of samples can be intrinsically degrading because employees will need to remove their outer clothing and urinate in secure rooms or lavatories in which the water supply has been turned off. Another person may have to be present at the test to ensure there is no specimen-tampering. Laboratory procedures can also entail invasions of personal privacy. Urinalysis reveals not only the presence of illegal drugs, but also the existence of many other physical and medical conditions, including genetic predisposition to disease, the use of prescription drugs, and pregnancy.

Aside from the issues of privacy and data protection, there is a compelling argument that both laboratory staff and employers are under a duty of confidentiality not to disclose these incidental matters to a third party. Guidelines published on behalf of the Home Office recommend that companies wanting to test should bear in mind the acronym JAPAN – that testing should be justifiable, auditable, proportionate, accountable and necessary.

It should also be remembered that an employee who has been asked by the employer to undergo medical screening without a reasonable and proper cause may succeed in arguing that the employer's conduct has destroyed or seriously damaged the relationship of mutual trust and confidence between them, thus entitling him or her to bring an unfair constructive dismissal claim.

19.2. Checklist of Do's and Don'ts

- Adopt a clear policy on dealing with drugs and alcohol in the workplace.
- Ensure that such matters as drug and alcohol testing, driving bans, drug taking outside work, criminal offences, etc., are dealt with in the drug and alcohol policy.
- Don't ignore the possibility that an employee may be suffering from a disability within the meaning of the DDA and need to be dealt with under ill-health procedures first, even if the employee has committed an act of misconduct.
- Even where an employee has committed an act of misconduct, a reasonable investigation may require an employer to obtain medical advice.

20. AIDS, HIV, SARS, BLOODBORNE PATHOGENS

20.1. Overview

There are no specific employment laws in England providing protection for employees with AIDS, HIV, SARS, or bloodborne pathogens, except that HIV is deemed to be a disability within the meaning of the EA 2010, and therefore discrimination against employees with HIV is prohibited (see disability discrimination above). Other conditions may satisfy the definition of disability within the meaning of the EA 2010.

20.2. Checklist of Do's and Don'ts

When taking any action in relation to employees with such conditions, seek medical advice to ascertain whether the condition falls within the meaning of disability.

21. DRESS AND GROOMING REQUIREMENTS

21.1. Overview

Employers can establish standards of dress and grooming. It is, however, good practice to ensure that such standards are set out clearly in a policy or staff handbook.

There are no specific employment laws in England and Wales relevant to issue of dress but issues of discrimination have arisen in a number of cases, for example where:

- an employer imposed different requirements between men and women, in particular that men were required to wear a shirt and tie whereas women were not;[7]
- an employer required a female Muslim language support teacher to remove her veil when teaching;[8]
- as part of its uniform policy, an employer prohibited all items of jewellery being displayed visibly to the public.[9]

21.2. Checklist of Do's and Don'ts

- When adopting standards of dress, ensure that such standards are set out in a policy.
- Assess dress standards for their potential discriminatory effect.
- Ensure that dress requirements and any refusal to allow an item of dress or jewellery as part of a religion or belief can be objectively justified.
- Ensure that any complaint by an employee be considered very carefully as part of a grievance procedure.

22. PRIVACY, TECHNOLOGY AND TRANSFER OF PERSONAL DATA

22.1. Privacy Rights of Employees

With the massive growth of the Internet and the fact that so much communication is now done by e-mail, more employers want to monitor their employees' use of e-mail and Internet, and even intercept e-mails. Such matters raise issues of privacy and data protection.

---

7. In Department for Work and Pensions v. Thompson, the court held that an employer's overarching requirement that all staff dress in a professional and business-like way could lawfully be achieved by imposing different conditions, in terms of specific items of dress, on men and women.
8. In Azmi v. Kirklees Metropolitan Borough Council a female Muslim teacher lost her discrimination case when the court concluded that the requirement to remove her veil was justified.
9. In Eweida v. British Airways plc a uniform policy operated by the company prohibiting items of jewellery, and in this case the claimant's crucifix, being displayed visibly to the public was not justified.

Is There a Right to Privacy at Work?

There is no freestanding right to privacy under UK law. However, the Human Rights Act (HRA) 1998 was introduced to give effect in the UK to the rights guaranteed under the European Convention for the Protection of Human Rights and Fundamental Freedoms ('the convention'). Amongst the many rights provided under the convention is a respect for private life (Article 8) guarantees of freedom of thought (Article 9) guarantees of freedom of expression (Article 10).

The HRA 1998 is only directly enforceable against public authorities. However, the definition of public authority is broad, including any person who carries out functions of a 'public nature' and this includes the Employment Tribunal, which must take into account the HRA when considering employment claims.

An action cannot be pursued against a private entity on the basis of a breach of the HRA alone, such as a breach of privacy.

Monitoring Employees

Employers who wish to monitor the use by its workers of its electronic communications, including the Internet and e-mail, must comply with various legislation, including the Data Protection Act 1998 (DPA), the Regulation of Investigatory Powers Act 2000 (RIPA), the Telecommunications (Lawful Business Practice) (Interception of Communications) Regulations 2000 and the convention as incorporated into UK law by the HRA.

In addition to the above-mentioned legislative provisions, when monitoring and collecting private information about staff, an employer must have regard to general principles of fairness. If information is collected in a particularly intrusive way there may be a risk that the employer's actions will fundamentally undermine the relationship of trust and confidence with its employees. This could allow an employee to resign in response to a breach of the implied term that neither party to an employment contract will do anything to damage the mutual trust and confidence between employer and employee and pursue a claim for constructive unfair dismissal.

Monitoring is not limited to checking Internet and e-mail and may include CCTV, monitoring telephone calls, tracking devices in vehicles and gathering information through point of sale terminals.

Data Protection Act 1998

The DPA governs how personal data about individuals (the 'data subject') can be handled by those individuals or companies who administer personal data (the 'data controller') It often applies to information held by employers on their workers. The DPA and the eight data protection principles are relevant to monitoring and what an employer can do with information obtained via monitoring.

The eight data protection principles require that personal information must be:

- Fairly and lawfully processed.
- Processed for limited purposes.
- Adequate, relevant and not excessive.
- Accurate and up-to-date.
- Not kept for longer than is necessary.
- Processed in line with the data subject's rights.
- Secure.
- Not transferred to other countries without adequate protection.

The DPA does not prevent monitoring. Indeed in some cases monitoring might be necessary to satisfy its requirements. However, any adverse impact of monitoring on individuals must be justified by the benefits to the employer and others.

In addition, the DPA has led to the publication of the Information Commissioner's Employment Practices Code (the 'Employment Code'), compliance with which will be taken into account in any enforcement action under the DPA.

In essence, under the DPA and the Employment Code, proportionality and the provision of full information to workers are central to any assessment of whether monitoring is justified.

Is Monitoring Proportionate?

Proportionality requires an employer to balance the reasons for monitoring against the impact on the employee. In particular, the employer has to consider whether such reasons are sufficient to justify an intrusion into an employee's private life, and whether the means of monitoring chosen are proportionate to meet that need.

The Employment Code recommends that employers undertake 'impact assessments' to demonstrate that they have achieved the desired balance between allowing workers to enjoy privacy in the workplace, and ensuring that the interests of the business are protected. According to Part 3 of the Employment Code an impact assessment involves:

- identifying clearly the purpose(s) behind the monitoring arrangement and the benefits it is likely to deliver;
- identifying any likely adverse impact of the monitoring arrangement;
- considering alternatives to monitoring or different ways in which it might be carried out;
- taking into account the obligations that arise from monitoring;
- judging whether monitoring is justified.

The Provision of Full Information

The second key theme in terms of DPA compliance and monitoring is the provision of full information to workers about any monitoring. The standard is high. For example, the Supplementary Guidance to Part 3 of the Employment Code states it is not enough to simply tell employees that their e-mail is being monitored. Employees must have a clear understanding of when information about their e-mail use will be obtained, why it is being obtained, how this information will be used and who it will be disclosed to.

Consent

Generally, an employer will not need an employee's specific consent to monitor, provided that it has conducted an impact assessment. However, the employee has to consent to monitoring or processing of any sensitive personal data, such as data relating to racial or ethnic origin, political opinions, religious beliefs and physical or mental health. Obtaining consent however does not absolve an employer from the need to comply with the requirement to perform the balancing act referred to above.

New Data Protection Legislation

A new Data Protection Act 2018 is expected to come into force during 2018 which will incorporate into UK law the EU General Data Protection Regulations (GDPR), due to come into force on 25 May 2018. The GDPR strengthens the rights of data subjects, requires data controllers to be more explicit in explaining how they use personal data (by the introduction of privacy notices) and has tightened the rules on consenting to processing personal data, particularly by allowing data subjects to withdraw consent at any time.

22.2. Checklist of Do's and Don'ts

- Ensure that all employees are aware of the policy on the use of electronic communications which sets out clearly to employees the circumstances in which they may or may not use the employer's telephone systems (including mobile phones), e-mail system and Internet access for private communications.
- Before monitoring private communications, carry out an impact assessment to ensure that any monitoring is proportionate, the reason for monitoring justifies the means and the least intrusive method is used.

- Ensure that employees are aware of any monitoring of phone calls, e-mails and Internet access. Employees should be told if such communications are going to be monitored and why.
- In assessing whether the monitoring of content is justified, employers should take into account the privacy of those sending the e-mails as well as the privacy and autonomy of those receiving them.

23. WORKPLACE INVESTIGATIONS FOR COMPLAINTS OF DISCRIMINATION, HARASSMENT, FRAUD, THEFT AND WHISTLEBLOWING

23.1. Overview

There are no statutory obligations or requirements of employers concerning workplace investigations, except that if there are complaints about how an investigation has been handled or conducted, it may be challenged by a dismissed employee and provide grounds for an unfair dismissal claim.

23.2. Checklist of Do's and Don'ts

- Investigation procedures should be set out in policies on harassment, whistleblowing, grievance and disciplinary hearings.
- Managers should be trained in conducting investigations.

24. AFFIRMATIVE ACTION/NON-DISCRIMINATION REQUIREMENTS

24.1. Overview

Commission for Equality and Human Rights

On 1 October 2007, the Commission for Equality and Human Rights came into existence. This non-departmental public body was established under the Equality Act 2006 which received Royal Assent on 16 February 2007. It has since rebranded itself as the Equality and Human Rights Commission (EHRC). The EHRC aims to promote equality and combat discrimination. Its duties are to:

- promote understanding of the importance of equality and diversity;
- encourage good practice in relation to equality and diversity;

- enforce the equality enactments and promote awareness and understanding of rights under them;
- promote equality of opportunity;
- work towards the elimination of unlawful discrimination and harassment.

The EHRC has a duty to monitor the effectiveness of all equality and human rights laws, make recommendations and provide advice to both central and devolved government. This will include advice on the likely effect of proposed changes in the law.

The EHRC has the power to issue codes of practice to ensure compliance with the equality enactments as well as to promote equality of opportunity. Codes of practice are important because, although a breach of a code does not of itself make a person liable to criminal or civil proceedings, the codes will be admissible as evidence in discrimination proceedings. A tribunal must take a code of practice into account, where relevant.

The Equality Act 2006 gives the EHRC the power to conduct an inquiry relating to its duties. Inquiries are concerned with broad issues, such as:

- looking into the causes of inequality; and
- looking at the employment of protected people in particular sectors, for example, looking at the employment of disabled people in the retail sector.

The EHRC has the power to conduct investigations when it suspects that a person has committed an unlawful act of discrimination. Suspicion as to the commission of an unlawful act may arise from cases being heard in courts or tribunals, as a result of reports to the EHRC from victims of harassment or discrimination, from trade unions, as well as from inquiries conducted by the EHRC itself.

Before conducting an investigation, the EHRC must draw up terms of reference and give the person being investigated the opportunity to make representations. A draft report setting out conclusions must later be published by the EHRC. The findings in the report following an investigation is admissible (but not conclusive) evidence before a court or tribunal.

Following an investigation, the EHRC may serve a notice on a person, once it is satisfied that the person has committed an unlawful act. The notice may specify that the person must prepare an action plan in order to avoid the repetition or continuation of the unlawful act; it may also recommend action to meet these ends. The person to whom the unlawful act notice applies then has six weeks in which to appeal to a court or tribunal, on either of the following grounds:

- He has not committed the unlawful act specified in the notice.
- Where asked to prepare an action plan, it is unreasonable to do so.

Where the EHRC thinks an organization has committed an unlawful act (whether or not it has conducted an investigation), it may enter into a binding agreement with the organization. The organization must undertake not to commit an unlawful act (or take positive steps to that end) and, in exchange, the EHRC will refrain from taking enforcement action against it. However, such an agreement will be subject to variation or termination at any time and does not prevent the EHRC from applying to a court for an injunction restraining a person from committing an unlawful act or an order requiring a person to comply with an undertaking.[10]

Public Sector Duties

Public bodies have a statutory duty to promote equality of opportunity and to eliminate gender, race and disability discrimination. Under the Equality Act 2006, the EHRC may carry out an assessment of the extent to which a public body has complied with these duties. The EHRC may also apply to a court for an injunction against a public body to ensure compliance with its statutory duties.

In July 2008 the Government announced plans to introduce a new equality duty in 2011. This will cover all seven equality strands, namely race, disability, gender, gender identity, religion/belief, age, and sexual orientation.

Positive Action/Discrimination

'Positive discrimination' refers to the practice of giving an advantage to those groups in society which are often treated unfairly, usually because of their race, sex, sexual orientation, religion or disability. There is no prohibition on treating disabled people more favourably than non-disabled people. However, in relation to other strands of discrimination, the law takes a very restrictive line on positive discrimination.

The law currently allows only a limited form of positive discrimination, known as 'positive action'. There are two forms of positive action:

- Affording members of a disadvantaged group access to facilities for training which would help fit them for particular work.
- Encouraging members of a disadvantaged group to take advantage of opportunities for doing particular work.

To take advantage of the defence to discrimination, it will usually be necessary to show either that the group is under-represented in the work in question, or it is likely to have a particular disadvantage in taking up or doing that type of work.

10. Section 24 Equality Act 2006.

Positive action does not (at present) allow an employer to discriminate in the actual selection of the candidate for employment or promotion; (except selection based on disability) the selection of employees for dismissal; or the terms and conditions of employment. Although the EA 2010 has relaxed the laws on positive discrimination, it is somewhat doubtful that the new coalition government will bring the new provisions in the EA 2010 into force.

24.2. Checklist of Do's and Don'ts

- Adopt a system of equal opportunities monitoring so that unrepresented groups can be identified.
- Draft an action plan that specifies how certain goals contained in an equal opportunities policy are to be achieved, dealing with such matters as:
  (a) what will be done to achieve these goals;
  (b) which senior person is responsible for each action;
  (c) deadlines and targets for achieving the goals;
  (d) how breaches of the policy will be tackled and rectified;
  (e) how success or failure will be measured;
  (f) how, and how often, progress will be reviewed.

25. RESOLUTION OF LABOUR, DISCRIMINATION AND EMPLOYMENT DISPUTES: LITIGATION, ARBITRATION, MEDIATION AND CONCILIATION

25.1. Internal Dispute Resolution Processes

The ACAS code is intended to help employers and employees resolve grievances effectively in the workplace. Dealing with a grievance effectively can avert tribunal claims.

If an employee makes a successful claim in the employment tribunal but either the employer or the employee failed to follow the ACAS code, the level of compensation awarded to the employee may be affected. If the employer unreasonably failed to follow the Code, the tribunal may increase the employee's compensation by up to 25%. If the employee unreasonably failed to follow it, the tribunal may reduce their compensation by up to 25%.

A grievance can be any concern, problem or complaint that an employee raises with the employer. If a grievance cannot be resolved informally, the employee should raise it in writing with a manager (if the grievance concerns their line manager, the grievance should be raised with another manager).

A failure to raise the grievance in writing does not prevent an employee from bringing a tribunal claim about the matter. However, the employee may recover less compensation if they have not done so.

A meeting should be held to allow the employee to explain their grievance and how they think it should be resolved. Managers, employees and their companions should make every effort to attend the meeting. If the matter needs further investigation, the employer should consider adjourning the meeting and resuming it after the investigation has taken place. When the meeting is concluded, the employer should communicate its decision in writing without unreasonable delay, including (where appropriate) details of any action it intends to take to resolve the grievance.

25.2. Mediation and Conciliation

Mediation is a process used for resolving disputes in which a third person helps the parties negotiate a settlement. It concentrates on helping parties move from entrenched positions to finding a resolution to a dispute that is in their best interests. The parties retain responsibility for achieving a solution. In mediation the parties are put under pressure to find a settlement to their dispute, while the mediator, as a third party, manages or facilitates the process through which the parties get to a point where they can reach a settlement. However, the mediator does not impose any settlements.

ACAS has a legal duty to offer free conciliation where a complaint about employment rights has been made to an employment tribunal, and a power to provide conciliation where a claim could be made, but hasn't yet been so. The role of ACAS is to help find a solution that both sides find acceptable, instead of going to a tribunal hearing.

25.3. Arbitration

Arbitration involves an impartial outsider being asked to make a decision on a dispute. The arbitrator makes a firm decision on a case based on the evidence presented by the parties. Arbitration is voluntary, so both sides must agree to go to arbitration; they should also agree in advance that they will abide by the arbitrator's decision.

Arbitration can be seen as an alternative to a court of law with its rules for procedures such as disclosure of documents, evidence and so on. But arbitration is private rather than public. Unlike a court, in an arbitration hearing the Arbitrator will ask the questions. There is no formal cross-examination or swearing of oaths.

Arbitration is often used in collective employment related disputes. For example, a trade union might be in dispute with an employer over the annual pay rise. The union could agree with the employer to ask ACAS to appoint an independent arbitrator from its panel of arbitrators to hear the two sides' cases and then make an independent and impartial decision.

Arbitration can also be used to settle individual disputes. For example, an individual and an employer might decide to go to arbitration to avoid the stress and expense of an employment tribunal.

25.4. Litigation

Most employment disputes must be brought in the employment tribunal, although certain contractual claims, often high value ones, are often brought in the County and High Court. There are strict time limits that apply to the employment tribunal, requiring most claims to be brought within three months of the act complained about. For certain claims, such as unfair dismissal and breach of contract, the employment tribunal is restricted as to the maximum compensation it can award.

25.5. Fines, Penalties and Damages

The tribunal has the power to award unlimited compensation in discrimination cases and compensation up to the lower of twelve months' salary or the statutory cap in unfair dismissal cases. in unfair dismissal cases. In most cases, the bulk of compensation is made up of losses incurred by the unfair dismissal or act of discrimination. The employee is under a duty to mitigate any loss.

25.6. Checklist of Do's and Don'ts

Involve employees or their representatives in developing workplace procedures, and make sure those procedures are transparent and accessible to employees.

Train managers on how to handle grievances effectively, when to involve HR, and how to spot when there may be a potential legal claim.

Encourage managers to resolve issues pro-actively and informally before they get to a formal grievance stage.

Ensure that the grievance procedure is followed.

26. EMPLOYER RECORDKEEPING, DATA PROTECTION AND EMPLOYEE ACCESS TO PERSONNEL FILES AND RECORDS

26.1. Overview

The DPA governs the processing of personal data relating to employees. Although the DPA does not prevent an employer from collecting and maintaining the records it needs, employers may not be aware that the DPA will be relevant to their actions at each stage of employment.

Activities which amount to 'processing' for the purposes of the DPA include collecting, recording, organizing and storing data as well as retrieving, accessing, using, amending, altering, erasing, disclosing or destroying it. These forms of processing must all be carried out in accordance with the following eight data protection principles:

- Personal data shall be processed fairly and lawfully and, in particular, shall not be processed unless (a) at least one of the conditions in Schedule 2 of the DPA is met; and (b) in the case of sensitive personal data, at least one of the conditions in Schedule 3 is also met.
- Personal data shall be obtained for one or more specified and lawful purposes, and shall not be further processed in any manner incompatible with that purpose or those purposes.
- Personal data shall be adequate, relevant and not excessive in relation to the purpose or purposes for which they are processed.
- Personal data shall be accurate and, where necessary, kept up-to-date.
- Personal data processed for any purpose or purposes shall not be kept for longer than is necessary for that purpose or those purposes.
- Personal data shall be processed in accordance with the rights of data subjects under the DPA.
- Appropriate technical and organizational measures shall be taken against unauthorized or unlawful processing of personal data and against accidental loss or destruction of, and damage to, personal data.
- Personal data shall not be transferred to a country or territory outside the European Union unless that country or territory ensures an adequate level of protection for the rights and freedoms of data subjects in relation to the processing of personal data.

Schedule 2 Conditions

- The data subject has given their consent to the processing of personal data.
- The processing is necessary for the performance of a contract to which the data subject is a party.

- The processing is necessary for compliance with any legal obligation to which the data controller is subject, other than an obligation imposed by contract.
- The processing is necessary in order to protect the vital interests of the data subject.
- The processing is necessary for the administration of justice or the exercise of functions of a public nature.
- The processing is necessary for the purposes of legitimate interests pursued by the data controller or the third party or parties to whom the data are disclosed, except where the processing is unwarranted in any particular case by reason of prejudice to the rights and freedoms or legitimate interests of the data subjects.
- The processing is carried out in circumstances specified in an order made by the Secretary of State.

Schedule 3 Conditions

- The data subject has given their explicit consent to the processing of the personal data.
- The processing is necessary to exercise or perform any right or obligation conferred or imposed by law in connection with employment.
- The processing is necessary to protect the vital interests of the data subject (where their consent cannot reasonably be obtained) or of another person (where consent by the data subject has been unreasonably withheld).
- The processing is carried out in the course of the legitimate activities of a not-for-profit organization which exists for political, philosophical, religious or trade union purposes where the processing relates to a member or person in regular contact with the organization.
- The personal data have been made public deliberately by the data subject.
- The processing is necessary in connection with legal proceedings, to obtain legal advice or to exercise legal rights.
- The processing is necessary for the administration of justice or the exercise of functions of a public nature.
- The processing is necessary for medical purposes and is carried out by a health professional or someone owing an equivalent duty of confidentiality.
- Where the data relate to racial or ethnic origin, where the processing is necessary to review equality of opportunity and is carried out with appropriate safeguards.
- The processing is carried out in circumstances specified in an order made by the Secretary of State.

While it is not necessary to seek employees' prior consent to collect and retain most employment records, it is a fair processing requirement to inform employees of the purposes for which the data are intended to be processed. It is therefore good practice to prepare a fact sheet, or preferably a data protection policy, to inform employees about the sort of records that are being or are likely to be kept, the purposes for which they are retained and processed, and the circumstances in which they might be disclosed to third parties. Alternatively, this information could be included in the employer's staff handbook, on its intranet site or in its employment contracts.

There will of course be circumstances in which information relating to an employee may need to be disclosed to third parties and it is impractical to inform or seek consent from the employee. An example of this is where an employer wishes to disclose employee records to a potential purchaser of the business. The requirement to inform employees here may limit an employer's freedom of action in such an event. If an employer had obtained employees' consent to this possibility via their contracts at the outset of the employment relationship, then theoretically this consent may be sufficient to permit the disclosure.

26.2. Personnel Files

The DPA requires employers to process their employees' personal data 'fairly and lawfully'. This means (among other things) complying with at least one of the conditions in Schedule 2 to the DPA in respect of personal data and also, for sensitive personal data, one of the conditions in Schedule 3 to the DPA.

26.3. Confidentiality Rules

Employee records should be kept secure and the number of people with access to such records should be limited due to the confidential nature of the information contained in the records.

26.4. Employee Access

An employee may make a data subject access request as a result of which s/he will be entitled to be informed by their employer whether personal data is being processed about them and, if so, to be given a description of that data.

There is no obligation to provide a document (e.g., a letter or an e-mail) containing personal data. It is the information constituting the personal data contained in the document that must be supplied. The information should be provided in an intelligible and permanent form (e.g., paper) unless that is not possible or would involve disproportionate effort. If there are numerous e-mails, rather than printing them all off, it may be easier to copy them on to a CD or floppy disc. It is also permissible to create a new document just setting out the information which constitutes personal data. This may be appropriate if a document contains personal data on a third party, is particularly sensitive or lengthy, or includes irrelevant information.

An employer must comply with a data access request promptly and, in any case, within forty days of receipt of the request or, if later, within forty days of receipt of:

- a fee of GBP 10;
- evidence to confirm the identity of the individual; and
- any information necessary to locate the information sought.

If the employee concerned has previously made a similar request, the employer will only be obliged to respond if a reasonable interval of time has elapsed in the interim. Whether a further response should be provided will depend upon the circumstances, for example, whether the nature of the data is likely to have changed, and the employee's reason for making the request.

New Data Protection Legislation

A new Data Protection Act 2018 is expected to come into force during 2018 which will incorporate into UK law the EU General Data Protection Regulations (GDPR), due to come into force on 25 May 2018. The GDPR strengthens the rights of data subjects, requires data controllers to be more explicit in explaining how they use personal data (by the introduction of privacy notices) and has tightened the rules on consenting to processing personal data, particularly by allowing data subjects to withdraw consent at any time.

27. REQUIRED NOTICES AND POSTINGS

27.1. Overview

Not applicable.

27.2. Checklist of Do's and Don'ts

Not applicable.

28. BREXIT

The impact of Brexit on employment law is, on the face of it, likely to be limited. Although a significant proportion of UK employment law is derived from the EU, it is unlikely that there will be wholesale changes following Brexit. However, the government may take the opportunity to amend some areas to reduce regulatory burden on companies, including:

Amending or repealing the Agency Workers Regulations 2010.

Introducing a cap on compensation for discrimination similar to that for unfair dismissal.

Amending TUPE to make it more business friendly (for example, by making it easier to amend terms following a TUPE transfer).

Addressing the issue of whether employees accrue holiday while off sick.

Removing the cap on maximum weekly working hours.

The greatest practical implication for employers is the likely change to the right of freedom of movement following Brexit. There are currently large numbers of EU nationals living and working in the UK. A pragmatic arrangement may be for existing EU migrants to be able to stay in the UK (possibly until a certain date or for a limited period) on the basis that UK nationals working in the EU can do the same. Many EU nationals working here may be able to obtain permanent residence, or even British citizenship. Alternatively, EU nationals may be able to obtain permission to work in the UK in the same way as, for example, US nationals can do at the moment.

ENGLAND

ENGLAND

ENGLAND

ENGLAND

ENGLAND

Made in the USA
Monee, IL
13 September 2026

62974266R00070